Professional English in Use

Intermediate to advanced

ICT

Elena Marco Fabré
Santiago Remacha Esteras

CAMBRIDGE
UNIVERSITY PRESS

CAMBRIDGE UNIVERSITY PRESS
Cambridge, New York, Melbourne, Madrid, Cape Town,
Singapore, São Paulo, Delhi, Mexico City

Cambridge University Press
The Edinburgh Building, Cambridge CB2 8RU, UK

www.cambridge.org
Information on this title: www.cambridge.org/9780521685436

First published 2007
6th printing 2013

Printed and bound in the United Kingdom by the MPG Books Group

A catalogue record for this publication is available from the British Library

ISBN 978-0-521-68543-6 Student's Book

Produced by eMC Design Ltd, www.emcdesign.org.uk

Thanks

The authors wish to thank Alison Silver for her invaluable feedback and for editing the typescript.

Our special thanks to Chris Capper, commissioning editor, for his vision, support and faith in the project.

We must also thank Tamora James for her advice on technical aspects, and the team who assisted us in preparing the CIC electronic files: Ann Fiddes and Charlotte Broom. Thanks also to Lucy Hollingworth for her work on the Index.

The authors and publishers are grateful to the following teachers who reviewed and piloted the material throughout its development: Tim Banks, Emma Hilton, Ellen Rosenbaum.

Picture research by Suzanne Williams.

Proofreading by Ruth Carim.

Development of this book has made use of the Cambridge International Corpus (CIC). The CIC is a computerized database of contemporary spoken and written English, which currently stands at one billion words (see page 7).

Contents

WORD BUILDING

TYPICAL LANGUAGE FUNCTIONS IN ICT ENGLISH

Cambridge International Corpus

In writing this book, use has been made of related material from the Cambridge International Corpus.

The Cambridge International Corpus (CIC) is a very large collection of English texts, stored in a computerized database, which can be searched to see how English is used. It has been built up by Cambridge University Press over the last ten years to help in writing books for learners of English. The English in the CIC comes from newspapers, best-selling novels, non-fiction books on a wide range of topics, websites, magazines, junk mail, TV and radio programmes, recordings of people's everyday conversations and many other sources. The CIC currently stands at one billion words.

- The Corpus helps us to get a representative picture of how English is used, both in writing and in speech.

- It is constantly being updated so we are able to include new words in our books as soon as they appear.

- It is 'real' English so we can ensure that examples in our books are natural and realistic.

Professional English in Use

Professional English in Use ICT is part of a new series of **Professional English in Use** titles from Cambridge University Press. These books offer vocabulary reference and practice for specialist areas of professional English. Have you seen some of the other titles available in the series?

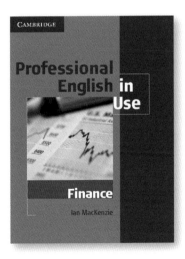
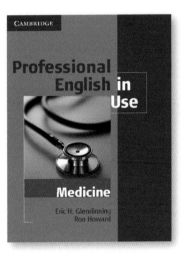
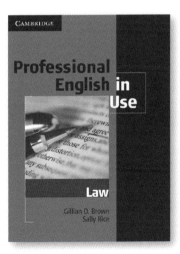

Introduction

Who is this book for?

ICT stands for Information Communications Technology, and describes the technologies we use in our daily lives to communicate. This book therefore looks particularly at the language of computing and the Internet but you'll also find topics such as mobile phones and video conferencing.

Professional English in Use ICT is designed for **intermediate to advanced level learners** who need to use the English of computing and the Internet for **study and work**. Computers have evolved so quickly that thousands of new jargon words are used to describe devices that didn't exist before. That's why this book is also suitable for people who use computers **at home** and want to improve their general knowledge of English and computers.

You can use this book on your own for **self-study**, or you can use it with a teacher **in the classroom.**

Why study ICT Vocabulary?

There are social, linguistic and educational reasons for studying this type of language.

Just read the technical specifications of your PC or explore a few websites and you will soon realize that **English is the language of computers and the Internet.** For example, lots of professionals, from engineers to desktop publishers, have to read technical documentation in English. In fact, in many companies English has become essential for working with computers. Besides, ICT English offers peculiar vocabulary, syntax and discourse **functions** that can be beneficial for developing your linguistic competence.

We hope this book will facilitate your interaction with computers and help you communicate more effectively in this digital world.

How is the book organized?

The book contains:
- **40 thematic units** plus **one introductory unit,** each occupying two pages. The left-hand page presents and explains ICT lexical areas. The right-hand page allows you to practise and extend your vocabulary.
- An **answer key** to the exercises.
- An **index,** which lists all the words and phrases introduced in the book, with the unit numbers where they appear; it also shows you how they are pronounced.

The units cover a wide range of topics from multimedia PCs and Internet issues to mobile phones and robots. It does not, however, require specialist knowledge of computers on either the part of the learner or teacher.

How are the units sequenced?

The introductory unit provides learners with some tips and techniques for learning vocabulary. Then the topics go from computers today to computers tomorrow. Unit 1 is about living with computers; Units 2–9 deal with hardware components; Unit 10 with health and safety; Units 11–18 with software and jobs in computing; Units 19–29 range from computer networks and the Web to e-commerce; Units 30–32 are about future developments; Units 33–36 deal with word-formation processes and collocations. Finally, Units 37–40 focus on some typical language functions in ICT English.

The left-hand page

This page introduces the **new words and expressions** for the unit. It is divided into **sections** indicated by letters (A, B, C), with simple, clear titles. Lexis is presented, and shown in **bold,** using different techniques:
- A short definition of a computer term
- A paragraph explaining an ICT concept or describing a computer device
- A diagram or picture illustrating a technical process, how computers work, etc.
- A situation where some words and uses are presented in context
- An authentic or adapted text from an original source

The right-hand page

This page contains **exercises** to practise the lexical items presented on the left-hand page.

Sometimes the exercises concentrate on using words presented on the left-hand page in typical contexts. Other exercises take the form of a crossword or other type of puzzle, or a diagram, which will help you remember computer terms.

There are also matching exercises and word-building activities which revise the use of prefixes, suffixes and compounds. Some units contain true/false exercises and texts to complete.

In some exercises you will be asked to recognize the new word in order to do a task.

A lot of the sentences are taken from the Cambridge International Corpus, from computer magazines and from websites, so they are related to the learner's own experience.

'You and computers' activities

These are an important feature of the book. The main aim is to personalize and develop the language in the unit. There are two types of activities:

- *Follow-up activities*
  These give you the chance to put into practice the words studied in the unit, and to develop your language skills by writing about or discussing topics relating to your studies or professional situation.
  Self-study learners can do these as written work. In the classroom, they can be done as a speaking activity.
- *Activities based on the* Professional English in Use ICT *website*
  These are based on links to external websites which have been carefully selected for their interesting topics and accessible language. You will be asked to look up words, give definitions, answer reading comprehension questions, etc. Answers are provided on the *Professional English in Use ICT* website. See www.cambridge.org/elt/ict.

Cartoons

The **cartoons** about computers and the Internet are intended to liven up the technical content of the book. We hope you enjoy them!

How should I use this book?

- The book presents ICT topics in a gradual development, from computer essentials to more sophisticated issues, so we recommend that you go through the units in sequential order. This will help you understand the basic aspects first and then proceed to more complex matters like networks.
- You may prefer to study only those units you are interested in. For example, you may want to focus on particular units like Internet security and online banking.
- A third possibility is to use the Index at the back of the book. You can use it to look for specific ICT terms and then go directly to the units in which they appear.

Don't forget!

- Use a notebook or a file on disk to write down important words and expressions.
- The *Professional English in Use ICT* website at www.cambridge.org/elt/ict gives you more opportunities to develop your knowledge through the Web. The site is related to *Infotech*, a comprehensive English course for computer users, by Santiago Remacha Esteras, published by Cambridge University Press.
- If you need access to a dictionary, you can visit the Cambridge dictionaries website at www.dictionary.cambridge.org or an online computer dictionary on the Web, e.g. www.webopedia.com.

0 Learning vocabulary: tips and techniques

A Guessing meaning from context

Some ICT terms are difficult, but others are universally accepted. You probably know terms like *modem*, *online*, *chat*, *email*, *website*, *virus* and *hacker*; they are part of our everyday life.

When you meet an unknown word, first try to guess the meaning from the context – the surrounding words and the situation.

Read the text on the right and see how words have meaning in relation to other words.

■ You know that a *PC* is a type of 'computer' and *digital music* relates to 'music on computers'.

■ You can guess that *are digitizing* is a verb because it derives from 'digit', it is in the form of the present continuous, and it goes with the subject 'families' and the object 'home movies'.

■ Words change their shape by adding prefixes and suffixes; for example, we add the prefix *inter-* to *net* and form *Internet*, and we add the suffix *-age* to *store* and form *storage*. (See Units 33 and 34.)

The birth of a revolution

Kids use PCs to do homework, access information via the <u>Internet</u> for research, communicate with pals, play video games and collect <u>digital music</u>. Parents, too, use the <u>PC</u> for communication and entertainment but also let it handle mundane tasks like balancing the checkbook, monitoring investments, preparing tax returns, and tracking the family's genealogy. With the advent of more powerful PCs with greater <u>storage</u> capacity, families <u>are digitizing</u> home movies and photos are stored on the home computer.   *Miami Herald*

B Organizing vocabulary

Read the text again. You can organize words in your notebook in different ways.

	How?	**Examples**
■ Meaning	definition	*The Internet is a global network of computers.*
	lexical family	*digit (root), digital, digitally, digitize, digitizer, digitized*
	synonyms	*handle = manage; advent = arrival*
	translation	*storage = almacenamiento (Spanish)*
■ Word class	(n), (v), (adj), etc.	*communication (n); communicate (v)*
■ Word building	prefixes	<u>Inter</u>net; <u>re</u>search
	suffixes	*inform<u>ation</u>; invest<u>ment</u>; power<u>ful</u>*
	compounds	*chequebook (cheque + book)*
■ Collocations	word partners, phrases	*access information; handle tasks*

> BrE: chequebook
> AmE: checkbook

Word trees and spidergrams can help you build up your own mental maps of vocabulary areas. You can make diagrams to classify things.

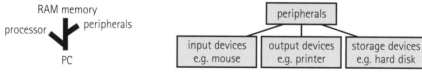

C Using a dictionary

A monolingual dictionary gives you a lot of information about words. Look at this entry.

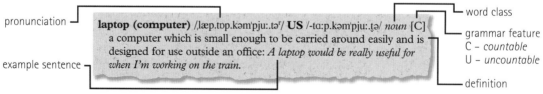

Use a bilingual dictionary if you find it easier. You may like to look at some Cambridge dictionaries at www.dictionary.cambridge.org. For ICT, you can also use an online computer dictionary.

(Cambridge Advanced Learner's Dictionary)

0.1 Look at the words in the box. Are they nouns, verbs or adjectives?

> financial   Internet   electronic   print   design   microchips

0.2 Read A opposite. Complete this text with words from exercise 1. Use the context to help you.

0.3 Match the words in exercise 1 with the following definitions.

1 tiny pieces of silicon containing complex electronic circuits
2 to make or draw plans for something
3 relating to money or how money is managed
4 involving the use of electric current in devices such as TV sets or computers
5 the large system of connected computers around the world
6 to produce text and pictures using a printer

A digital era

Computers have changed the way we do everyday things, such as working, shopping and looking for information. We (1) .... houses with the help of PCs; we buy books or make flight reservations on the (2) .... ; we use gadgets that spring to life the instant they are switched on, for example the mobile phone, the music player, or the car ignition, all of which use (3) .... Many people now work at home, and they communicate with their office by computer and telephone. This is called 'teleworking'.

With the appropriate hardware and software, a PC can do almost anything you ask. It's a magical typewriter that allows you to type and (4) .... any sort of document. It's a calculating machine that makes (5) .... calculations. It's a filing cabinet that manages large collections of data. It's a personal communicator that lets you interact with friends. It's a small lab that helps you edit photos and movies. And if you like (6) .... entertainment, you can also use it to relax with games.

0.4 Organize these words as in B opposite.

> mobile phone   interact   communicator   teleworking
> calculating   calculations   typewriter

- **Meaning**   definition   (1) .... : working at home, while communicating with your office by computer or telephone

  lexical family   calculate, calculator, (2) .... (3) ....
  synonyms   gadgets = small devices
  translation   switch on = (4) ....
- **Word building**   prefixes   (5) ....
  suffixes   (6) ....
  compounds   (7) .... (8) ....
- **Collocations**   word partners   print a document; make calculations

0.5 Look at this dictionary entry. Put these labels in the correct place.

1 pronunciation   3 example sentence   5 word class
2 definition   4 grammar feature

a ....   b ....   c ....

data /ˈdeɪ.tə/ US /-t̬ə/ *group noun* [U]
information, especially facts or numbers, collected for examination and consideration and used to help decision-making, or information in an electronic form that can be stored and processed by a computer: *The data was/were collected by various researchers. Now the data is being transferred from magnetic tape to hard disk.*

d ....

e ....

(Cambridge Advanced Learner's Dictionary)

You and computers

Find a dictionary and look up the meaning of these words.   1 hardware   2 software

1 Living with computers

A Computers: friend ...

People who have grown up with PCs and microchips are often called the digital generation. This is how some people answered when questioned about the use of computers in their lives.

> 'I have a **GPS**, **Global Positioning System**, fitted in my car. With this navigation system I never get lost. And the **DVD recorder** is perfect for my children's entertainment.'

> 'I use an **interactive whiteboard**, like a large touchscreen monitor, at school. I find computers very useful in education.'

> 'Assistive technology, for people with disabilities, has helped me a lot. I can hardly see, so I use a **screen reader**, a program that reads aloud onscreen text, menus and icons.'

> 'This new **HMD, head-mounted display**, allows me to watch films, and enjoy **virtual reality**, the artificial environment of the latest video games.'

> 'The upgraded **wireless network** at my university is great: we can connect our laptops, PDAs and Wi-Fi cell phones to the network anywhere in the campus. Communication is becoming easier and easier.'

B ... or foe?

- Our society has developed **technological dependence**. When computers are down, our way of life breaks down: planes stop flying, telephones don't work, banks have to close.
- Computers produce **electronic waste**, plastic cases and microchips that are not biodegradable and have to be recycled or just thrown away.
- They are responsible for health problems, e.g. **computer addiction**, an inappropriate and excessive use of computers.
- **Cybercrime**, crime committed with the help of computers, is creating serious problems.
- Citizens may feel a **loss of privacy** because of unauthorized use of personal data or receiving unwanted electronic messages.

C Things we can do on the computer

A publication

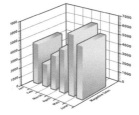

A business graph

Web pages and email

Photo editing

A secretary: 'I use computers to do the usual office things like **write letters** and **faxes**, but what I find really useful is email. We are an international company and I **send emails** to our offices all over the world.'

A publisher: 'We use PCs to produce all sorts of texts in digital format. We **publish e-books** (electronic books) and interactive e-learning programs on CD, and we help a local company to **design** an **online newspaper**, displayed on the Web.'

A bank manager: 'We use financial software to **make calculations** and then generate graphs or charts. We also use a database to **store information** so that it can be easily searched.'

A home user: 'I like to **retouch photos** on my computer; I improve them by making a few touches and then save them on a CD. I also enjoy looking at music portals on the Web. I **surf the Web** every day and I often **download files**, I copy music files from the Net to my PC.'

1.1 Complete these sentences with words from A opposite.

1 The .... is a piece of software that interfaces with your PC and allows you, via keyboard commands, to get any text information read to you in synthetic speech.

2 A ....-...................................... , as popularized by virtual reality, lets the user immerse him/herself in a synthetically generated environment.

3 An .... is a touch-sensitive device where a special pen or your finger can act as a mouse.

4 Tony Adams is now the proud owner of a dark silver Vogue, complete with leather interior, ... navigation, and a .... with LCD TV screens.

1.2 Which computer use in A do these pictures illustrate?

1.3 Read B opposite. What problem do these sentences refer to?

1 We are sorry to announce that most flights are delayed or cancelled.
2 He should go to a psychologist. He spends hours surfing the Web.
3 Technology changes so quickly that we have to scrap computers when they become obsolete.
4 I've been getting emails about offers for lots of different products.
5 My computer system has been broken into and some useful information has been destroyed.

1.4 Some words often appear together in IT. Complete these computer uses with word partners from C opposite.

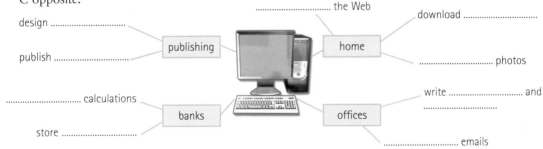

Computer and man both thinking "Stupid Idiot!"

You and computers

Make a list of the ways you use computers at work and in your free time.

2 A typical PC

A Computer essentials

monitor
webcam
software, e.g. word processor
speaker
CD/DVD drive
CPU (inside) Central Processing Unit
speaker
printer
keyboard
mouse
modem

B Parts of a computer

A computer is an electronic machine that accepts, processes, stores and outputs information. A typical computer consists of two parts: hardware and software.

Hardware is any electronic or mechanical part of the computer system that you can see or touch.

Software is a set of instructions, called a program, which tells a computer what to do. There are three basic hardware sections.

1 The **CPU** is the heart of the computer, a microprocessor chip which processes data and coordinates the activities of all the other units.

2 The **main memory** holds the instructions and data which are being processed by the CPU. It has two main sections: **RAM** (random access memory) and **ROM** (read only memory).

3 **Peripherals** are the physical units attached to the computer. They include:
Input devices, which let us enter data and commands (e.g. the keyboard and the mouse).
Output devices, which let us extract the results (e.g. the monitor and the printer).
Storage devices, which are used to store information permanently (e.g. hard disks and DVD-RW drives).
Disk drives are used to read and write data on disks.

At the back of a computer there are **ports** into which we can plug external devices (e.g. a scanner, a modem, etc.). They allow communication between the computer and the devices.

USB connector   USB ports

C Functions of a PC: input, processing, output, storage

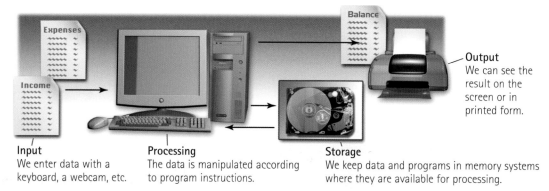

Balance
Expenses
Output
We can see the result on the screen or in printed form.
Income

Input
We enter data with a keyboard, a webcam, etc.

Processing
The data is manipulated according to program instructions.

Storage
We keep data and programs in memory systems where they are available for processing.

2.1 Look at A opposite. Read these quotations and say which computer essential they refer to.

1 'Accelerate your digital lifestyle by choosing a Pentium at 4.3 GHz.'
2 'Right-click to display a context-sensitive menu.'
3 'You will see vivid, detailed images on a 17" display.'
4 'This will produce high-quality output, with sharp text and impressive graphics.'
5 'Use it when you want to let the grandparents watch the new baby sleeping.'
6 'Press any key to continue.'

2.2 Match the terms with their definitions.

1 CD/DVD drive   a   any socket into which a peripheral device may be connected
2 speaker   b   device used to produce voice output and play back music
3 modem   c   mechanism that reads and/or writes to optical discs
4 port   d   device that converts data so that it can travel over the Internet

2.3 Look at B opposite and label this diagram with the correct terms.

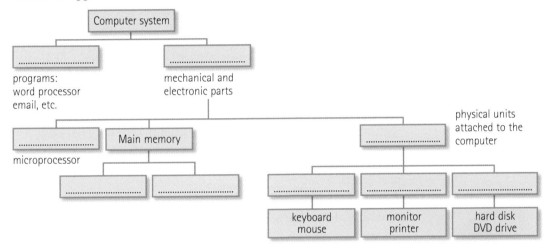

2.4 Complete the diagram and sentences below with words from C opposite.

1 Computer .... is the visible or audible result of data processing – information that can be read, printed or heard by the user.
2 The CPU will process data as instructed by the programs you're running. .... includes functions like calculating, sorting, editing, drawing and searching.
3 DVDs are expected to replace CDs as .... devices.
4 As a scanner, the Sigma-100 can be used to .... photographs as well as documents into the computer.

You and computers

Access the *Professional English in Use ICT* website at www.cambridge.org/elt/ict.
Then do the activity Computer history.

3 Types of computer systems

A From mainframes to wearable computers

A **mainframe** is the most powerful type of computer. It can process and store large amounts of data. It supports multiple users at the same time and can support more simultaneous processes than a PC. The central system is a large server connected to hundreds of terminals over a network. Mainframes are used for large-scale computing purposes in banks, big companies and universities.

A **desktop PC** has its own processing unit (or CPU), monitor and keyboard. It is used as a personal computer in the home or as a workstation for group work. Typical examples are the IBM PC and the Apple Macintosh. It's designed to be placed on your desk. Some models have a vertical case called a tower.

A **laptop** (also called a **notebook PC**) is a lightweight computer that you can transport easily. It can work as fast as a desktop PC, with similar processors, memory capacity, and disk drives, but it is portable and has a smaller screen. Modern notebooks have a **TFT** (Thin Film Transistor) **screen** that produces very sharp images.

Instead of a mouse, they have a **touchpad** built into the keyboard – a sensitive pad that you can touch to move the pointer on the screen.

They offer a lot of connectivity options: **USB** (Universal Serial Bus) **ports** for connecting peripherals, slots for memory cards, etc.

They come with **battery packs**, which let you use the computer when there are no electrical outlets available.

A **tablet PC** looks like a book, with an LCD screen on which you can write using a special digital pen. You can fold and rotate the screen 180 degrees. Your handwriting can be recognized and converted into editable text. You can also type at the detached keyboard or use voice recognition. It's mobile and versatile.

A **personal digital assistant** or **PDA** is a tiny computer which can be held in one hand. The term PDA refers to a wide variety of **hand-held** devices, palmtops and pocket PCs.

For input, you type at a small keyboard or use a **stylus** – a special pen used with a **touch screen** to select items, draw pictures, etc. Some models incorporate **handwriting recognition,** which enables a PDA to recognize characters written by hand. Some PDAs recognize spoken words by using **voice recognition** software.

They can be used as mobile phones or as personal organizers for storing notes, reminders and addresses. They also let you access the Internet via **wireless** technology, without cables.

A **wearable computer** runs on batteries and is worn on the user's body, e.g. on a belt, backpack or vest; it is designed for mobile or hands-free operation. Some devices are equipped with a wireless modem, a small keyboard and a screen; others are voice-activated and can access email or voice mail.

3.1 Look at A opposite. Which type of computer do these descriptions refer to?

1 a hand-held computer which can be used as a telephone, a web explorer and a personal organizer
2 a typical computer found in many businesses and popular for home use
3 a large computer used for intensive data processing and often linked to many terminals
4 a small computer that fits into items of clothing
5 a portable computer that can be closed up like a briefcase, but it can be as powerful as a desktop PC
6 a full-function PC, though it only weighs 1.2 kg – you can go to a meeting and write your notes on it, like a paper notepad; its screen mode can be changed from portrait to landscape

3.2 Look at the computer advertisement and find this information.

Toshiba Satellite
- Intel Centrino processor
- 1,024 MB RAM, 100 GB hard disk drive
- DVD SuperMulti (+/-R double layer) drive
- 15.4" widescreen TFT active-matrix LCD display
- 85-key keyboard and touchpad
- 2 memory slots, 1 PC Card or PCMCIA slot
- Wireless communications: Wi-Fi compliancy and Bluetooth
- 4 USB ports for connecting peripherals: digital camera, MP3 player, modem, etc.
- 6-cell rechargeable Lithium-ion battery pack

1 What type of computer is advertised?
2 What kind of screen does it have?
3 Which pointing device replaces the mouse?
4 What type of ports does it have for connecting cameras and music players?
5 What sort of power supply does it use?

3.3 Read this interview with Adam Hawkins, an IT manager, and complete it with words from the PDA section opposite.

Interviewer: What are the basic features of a PDA?
Adam: Well, a typical PDA is a (1) .... device that runs on batteries and combines computing, phone and Net capabilities.
Interviewer: And how do you enter information?
Adam: For input, you use a (2) .... or pen to write and make selections on a (3) .... ; they also have buttons for launching programs. Some models have a small keyboard. They may have a (4) .... system that reacts to the user's voice.
Interviewer: Do they need special software?
Adam: Yes, most of them run on *Windows Mobile*. Palmtops supported by Palm Inc. use *Palm OS*. Pen-based systems include (5) .... , so you write on the screen and the computer recognizes your handwriting and inserts the appropriate letters.
Interviewer: What sort of things can you do with a PDA?
Adam: You can store personal information, take notes, draw diagrams and make calculations. Many PDAs can access the Net via (6) .... technology.

You and computers

1 Write down two benefits and two limitations of PDAs.

2 Explain in a paragraph how laptops can be beneficial to business people.

3 Write three examples of how tablet PCs can be used in the classroom.

4 Input devices: type, click and talk!

Interacting with your computer

Input devices are the pieces of hardware which allow us to enter information into the computer.

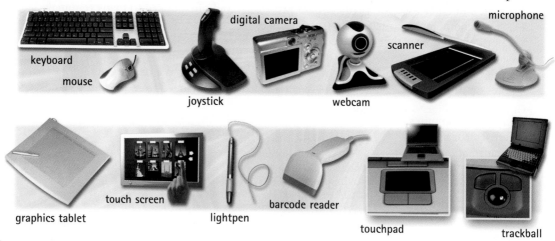

keyboard · mouse · joystick · digital camera · webcam · scanner · microphone

graphics tablet · touch screen · lightpen · barcode reader · touchpad · trackball

The keyboard

A standard PC keyboard has various groups of keys.

- **Alphanumeric keys** – these represent letters and numbers, arranged as on a typewriter.
- A **numeric keypad** appears to the right of the main keyboard and contains numeric and editing keys; the Num Lock key is used to switch from numbers to editing functions.
- **Function keys** appear at the top of the keyboard and can be programmed to do special jobs.
- **Cursor keys** include 'arrow keys' which move the insertion point, and keys such as Home, End, Page Up, and Page Down, which let you move around documents.
- **Dedicated keys** are used to issue commands or produce alternative characters. For example:
  Ctrl changes the functions of other keys (e.g. Ctrl + X cuts the selected text).
  Caps Lock sets the keyboard in 'CAPITALS' mode; it only affects letters.
  Enter (or **Return**) is pressed to select options from a menu or to start a new paragraph.
  Backspace deletes the character to the left of your current position.

The mouse

A mouse is a hand-held device that lets you move a pointer (or cursor) and select items on the screen. It has one or more buttons to communicate with the PC. A scroll wheel lets you move through your documents or web pages The pointer looks like an I-bar, an arrow or a pointing hand.

An optical mouse has an optical sensor instead of a ball underneath.

A cordless (wireless) mouse has no cable; it sends data via infrared signals or radio waves.

Mouse actions:

- to **click**, press and release the left button.
- to **double-click**, press and release the left button twice.
- to **drag**, hold down the button, move the pointer to a new place and then release the button.
- to **right-click**, press and release the right button; this action displays a list of commands.

Voice input

Today you can also interact with your computer by voice with a **voice-recognition system** that converts voice into text, so you can dictate text directly onto your word processor or email program. You can also control your PC with voice commands; this means you can launch programs, open, save or print files. Some systems let you search the Web or chat using your voice instead of the keyboard.

4.1 Look at A opposite. Which input device would you use for these tasks?

1 to play computer games
2 to copy images from paper into a computer
3 to read price labels in a shop
4 to select text and click on links on web pages
5 to enter drawings and sketches into a computer
6 to input voice commands and dictate text
7 to draw pictures or select menu options directly on the screen
8 to take and store pictures and then download them to a computer

4.2 Complete each sentence by choosing from the following devices: *touch screen, trackball, touchpad, webcam*.

1 A .... is a stationary device that works like a mouse turned upside down. You roll the ball with your hand to move the pointer on the screen.
2 Interactive .... are used in museums, information centres and Internet kiosks. You use your finger to point directly to objects on the screen.
3 A .... is used to send live video images via the Internet.
4 A .... is found on notebook PCs. You use it by pressing the sensitive pad with a finger.

4.3 Label the groups of keys with terms from B opposite. Then identify the keys described below.

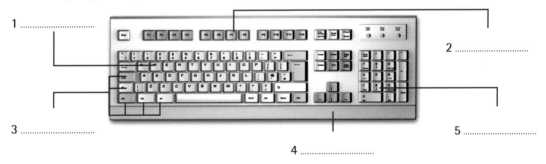

1 ....

2 ....

3 ....

4 ....

5 ....

6 It produces upper-case letters, but it does not affect numbers and symbols.
7 It removes the character to the left of the cursor or any selected text.
8 It works in combination with other keys, e.g. you press this key and C to copy the selected text.
9 It is used to confirm commands; in a word processor, it creates a new paragraph.

4.4 Look at C opposite. Complete these sentences with the correct 'mouse action'.

1 To start a program or open a document you .... on its icon – that is, you rapidly press and release the mouse button twice.
2 If you want to select a menu option, you just .... on the left button.
3 If you want to find the commands for a particular text, image, etc., you have to .... on it.
4 If you want to move an object, press the button and .... the object to the desired location.

You and computers

1 Read D opposite and make a list of the things you can do with a voice-recognition system.

2 What do you think of this idea? *Some day, we'll be talking to our PC naturally, like a friend.* Write down your opinions.

"That must be the new neighbor. I hear he's a real computer geek."

5 Input devices: the eyes of your PC

Scanners

Input devices such as scanners and cameras allow you to capture and copy images into a computer.

A **scanner** is a **peripheral** that reads images and converts them into electronic codes which can be understood by a computer. There are different types.

- A **flatbed** is built like a photocopier and is for use on a desktop; it can capture text, colour images and even small 3D objects.
- A **film scanner** is used to scan film negatives or 35 mm **slides** – pictures on photographic film, mounted in a frame.
- A **hand-held scanner** is small and T-shaped, ideal to capture small pictures and logos.
- A **pen scanner** looks like a pen; you can scan text, figures, barcodes and handwritten numbers.

A pen scanner

Barcode scanners read barcodes on the products sold in shops and send the price to the computer in the cash register. **Barcodes** consist of a series of black and white stripes used to give products a unique identification number.

The **resolution** of a scanner is measured in **dpi** or dots per inch. For example, a 1,200 dpi scanner gives clearer, more detailed images than a 300 dpi scanner.

Most scanners come with **Optical Character Recognition** software. OCR allows you to scan pages of text and save them into your word processor; they can then be edited.

Barcode and reader

Digital cameras

A **digital camera** doesn't use film. Photos are stored as digital data (bits made up of 1s and 0s), usually on a tiny storage device known as a **flash memory** card. You can connect the camera or memory card to a PC and then alter the images using a program like Adobe Photoshop, or you can view the images on a TV set. Many printers have a special socket so that you can print images directly from a memory card or camera.

Digital video cameras and webcams

INPUT
A **digital video (DV) camera** records moving images and converts them into digital data that can be processed by a PC.

PROCESSING
You can manipulate video images with **video editing software**. You can cut, paste, add effects, etc.

OUTPUT
You can store or export the result.

Display it on a screen or create a DVD.

File Edit Image Layer
WWW.

Email or put your movie on the Web.

Webcams (short for Web cameras) let you send and receive live video pictures through the Internet. They're primarily used for **video conferences** – video calls – but they can be used to record photos and video onto your hard disk.

The resolution of webcams is expressed in **megapixels** (million pixels). Webcams connect to the PC via a **USB** (universal serial bus) or FireWire port; they display video at 24 to 30 **frames** (pictures) per second. Some include a **headset** with a microphone and earpiece.

5.1 Solve the clues and complete the puzzle with words from A and B opposite.

1 Scanners and cameras are .... devices used to transfer images into a format that can be understood by computers.
2 A .... lets you copy photos and printed documents into your PC.
3 It has become one of life's most familiar sounds – the beep of the supermarket till whenever a .... is scanned.
4 If you need to scan 35mm .... you should go for a dedicated 35mm film scanner which concentrates all its dots into a tiny area.
5 This scanner has a resolution of 300 x 600 ....
6 A .... scanner is small enough to hold in your hand.
7 A .... scanner is used to capture lines of text, barcodes and numbers.
8 Most digital cameras use flash .... cards to store photos.
9 .... scanners have a flat surface and take at least A4-sized documents.
10 To scan photographic negatives or slides you will need a .... scanner.

The crossword grid spells vertically: p, e, r, i, p, h, e, r, a, l

5.2 Decide if these sentences are *True* or *False*. If they are false, correct them.

1 The details detected by a scanner are not determined by its resolution.
2 A barcode scanner is a computer peripheral for reading barcode labels printed on products.
3 Scanners cannot handle optical character recognition.
4 A digital camera uses a light sensitive film instead of a memory card for storing the images.
5 A digital video (DV) camera is used to take still photographs.
6 Video editing software allows you to manipulate video clips on the computer.

5.3 Complete this advertisement with words from the webcam section of C opposite.

Having (1) .... with friends and family has never been easier or more enjoyable. You get the highest-quality audio and video, no matter which chatting solution you use. With the WebCam Live! Ultra, its CCD image sensor with 640 x 480 (VGA) resolution produces rich, vibrant colours. Combined with its (2) .... 2.0 Hi-Speed connection, the result is top-quality, full-motion video at 30 (3) .... per second for all your web conversations, even in dimly-lit rooms.
The WebCam Live! Ultra lets you do more. Let your voice be heard clearer than ever before with the included (4) ...., unlike the built-in microphones in most other (5) .... Take still pictures at up to 1.3 (6) .... resolution (interpolated), and enjoy the many great features that accompany the bundled award-winning WebCam Center software, such as motion detection, remote security monitoring, timelapse video capture and much more.

You and computers

1 Write one reason for using a scanner at home or at work.
2 Do you have a digital camera? Describe its basic features and the things you do with it.

6 Output devices: printers

A Technical details

A **printer** is a device that prints your texts or graphics on paper.

The output on paper or acetate sheets is called **printout** or hard copy.

A program in your computer, called the **printer driver**, converts data into a form that your printer can understand.

A **print spooler** stores files to be printed when the printer is ready. It lets you change the order of documents in the queue and cancel specific print jobs.

The output quality, or **resolution**, is measured in **dpi** or dots per inch.

The speed of your printer is measured in **pages per minute (ppm).**

In a network, users can share a printer connected to a **print server**, a computer that stores the files waiting to be printed.

B Types of printers

A **dot-matrix printer** uses a group, or matrix, of **pins** to create precise dots. A print head containing tiny pins strikes an inked ribbon to make letters and graphics. This **impact printing** technology allows shops, for example, to print multi-part forms such as receipts and invoices, so it's useful when self-copying paper is needed. It has two important disadvantages: noise and a relatively low resolution (from 72 to 180 dpi).

A dot-matrix printer

An **ink-jet** (also called bubble-jet) **printer** generates an image by spraying tiny, precise drops of ink onto the paper. The resolution ranges from 300 to 1,200 dpi, suitable for small quantities or home use.

A standard ink-jet has a three-colour **cartridge**, plus a black cartridge. Professional ink-jets have five-colour cartridges, plus black; some can print in wide format, ranging from 60 cm up to 5 metres (e.g. for printing advertising graphics).

Some ink-jet based printers can perform more than one task. They are called **multi-function printers** because they can work as a scanner, a fax and a photocopier as well as a printer. Some units accept memory cards and print photos directly from a camera.

An ink-jet printer and ink cartridges

A **laser printer** uses a laser beam to fix the ink to the paper. A laser works like a photocopier; a powder called **toner** is attracted to paper by an electrostatic charge and then fused on by a hot roller.

Laser printers are fast and produce a high resolution of 1,200 to 2,400 dpi, so they are ideal for businesses and for proofing professional graphics work.

Lasers use a **page description language** or PDL which describes how to print the text and draw the images on the page. The best-known languages are Adobe PostScript and HP Printer Control Language.

A professional **imagesetter** is a typesetting printer that generates very high-resolution output (over 3,540 dpi) on paper or microfilm. It's used for high-quality publications.

A **plotter** is a special type of printer which uses ink and fine pens held in a carriage to draw detailed designs on paper. It's used in computer-aided design, maps, 3-D technical illustrations, etc.

A plotter

6.1 Complete these sentences with words from A opposite.

1 The differences in .... are noticeable: the more dots per inch, the clearer the image.
2 A print resolution of between 600 .... and 2,400 .... ensured that even text as small as 2 pt was legible.
3 Passengers with an electronic ticket will need a .... of ticket confirmation or a boarding pass to be admitted to secured gate areas.
4 The key advance of recent years is printing speed: the latest generation of ink-jets prints black-and-white text at 15 .... (............................).
5 With appropriate software, you can view the images on a computer, manipulate them, or send them to a .... and produce excellent quality colour copies.
6 A .... is a dedicated computer that connects a printer to a network. It enables users to share printing resources.
7 A .... is a utility that organizes and arranges any documents waiting to be printed.
8 In computers, a .... is a program installed to control a particular type of printer.

6.2 Choose the most appropriate type of printer for these situations from the descriptions in B opposite.

1 a home user who wants to print text documents and family photographs
2 business people who need to print in large quantities at high quality in an office
3 engineers who want to make detailed line drawings
4 professional typesetters in desktop publishing (e.g. to publish catalogues and magazines)
5 a company that wants to print carbon copies of bills and receipts

6.3 Find terms in B opposite which correspond to these definitions.

1 a container that holds the ink in an ink-jet printer
2 powdered ink used in laser printers
3 small needles that press on the inked ribbon to make the characters on paper
4 printer technology that produces text and pictures by hammering pins against a ribbon and the paper
5 a language that tells a printer how to print a document
6 a peripheral which combines a printer, a fax machine and photocopying and scanning capability into one device

Dangerous laser printers

You and computers

Describe the characteristics of the printer that you have or would like to have at home or at work.

Give details about: type of printer, speed, resolution, ink cartridges, price and customer support.

7 Output devices: display screens

CRTs and LCDs

The screen of a computer is often known as the **monitor**, or VDU (visual display unit). Inside the computer, there is a **video card** which processes images and sends signals to the monitor.

When choosing a monitor, you have to take into account a few basics.

- Type of display – the choice is between a **CRT** or an **LCD** screen.
  The **Cathode Ray Tube** of a monitor is similar to a traditional TV set. It has three electron guns (one for each **primary colour**: red, green and blue) that strike the inside of the screen, which is coated with substances called **phosphors**, which glow and create colours. CRTs are cheap, but they are heavy, can flicker and emit radiation.
  A **Liquid Crystal Display** is made from flat plates with a liquid crystal solution between them. The crystals block the light in different quantities to create the image. **Active-matrix** LCDs use TFT (thin film transistor) technology, in which each pixel has its own transistor switch. They offer better quality and take up less space, so they are replacing CRTs.

- **Screen size** – the viewing area is measured **diagonally**; in other words, a 17" screen measures 17 inches from the top left corner to the bottom right.

- **Resolution** – the clarity of the image depends on the number of **pixels** (short for picture elements) contained on a display, horizontally and vertically. A typical resolution is 1,024 x 768. The sharpness of images is affected by **dot pitch**, the distance between the pixels on the screen, so a dot pitch of 0.28 mm or less will produce a sharp image.

- **Brightness** – the luminance of images is measured in cd/m^2 (candela per square metre).

- **Colour depth** – the number of colours a monitor can display. For example, a VGA monitor produces 256 colours, enough for home use; a SuperVGA can produce up to 16.7 million colours, so is ideal for photographic work and video games.

- **Refresh rate** – the number of times that the image is drawn each second. If a monitor has a refresh rate of 75 Hertz (Hz), it means that the screen is scanned 75 times per second. If this rate is low, you will notice a flicker, which can cause eye fatigue.

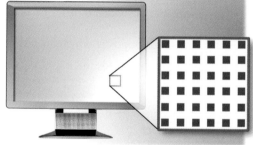

A colour pixel is a combination of red, green and blue subpixels

Big screens: plasma and projection TVs

'I sometimes use a video projector in my Geography lessons. I prepare audiovisual presentations on my laptop and then connect it to a **front-screen projector** which displays the images on a distant screen or white wall.'

'I am a **home cinema** enthusiast. I've set up a system with a DVD recorder, speakers for surround sound, and a **rear projection** TV, which has the video projector and the screen within a large TV box. It's a real cinema experience.'

'I use a portable DLP projector for my business presentations. This is a **digital light-processing** device which creates the image with millions of microscopic mirrors arranged on a silicon chip.'

'I've got a 52-inch **plasma display** and really enjoy its advantages: high-contrast images and bright colours, generated by a plasma discharge which contains noble, non-harmful gases. Gas-plasma TVs allow for larger screens and wide viewing angles, perfect for movies!'

7.1 Read A opposite and then correct these false statements.

1 The images shown on a monitor are not generated by the video card.
2 All visible colours can be made from mixing the three primary colours of red, yellow and blue.
3 Typical CRT-based displays occupy less space than LCD displays.
4 Active-matrix LCDs do not use a technology called thin film transistor or TFT.
5 The size of the screen is measured horizontally.

7.2 Match each term with the correct definition.

1	phosphors	a	the frequency at which a monitor renews its image, measured in Hz
2	LCD screen	b	a flat-panel display which works by emitting light through a special liquid
3	pixel	c	the space between a display's pixels
4	dot pitch	d	the smallest element in a displayed image
5	refresh rate	e	materials that emit light and produce colours when they are activated by an electron beam

7.3 Complete the technical specifications of this monitor with words from A opposite.

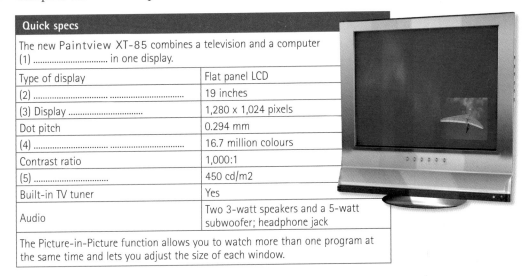

Quick specs	
The new Paintview XT-85 combines a television and a computer (1) .... in one display.	
Type of display	Flat panel LCD
(2)	19 inches
(3) Display	1,280 x 1,024 pixels
Dot pitch	0.294 mm
(4)	16.7 million colours
Contrast ratio	1,000:1
(5)	450 cd/m2
Built-in TV tuner	Yes
Audio	Two 3-watt speakers and a 5-watt subwoofer; headphone jack
The Picture-in-Picture function allows you to watch more than one program at the same time and lets you adjust the size of each window.	

7.4 Complete these sentences with words from B opposite.

1 If you intend to set up a .... , consider getting a very big screen, a DVD recorder and a good set of speakers.
2 A ....-.......................... .... takes digital images and displays them on a screen or wall.
3 The company announced plans to expand its ....-.......................... (DLP) cinema technology, which has thrilled test audiences with its dazzling colours and pin-sharp images.
4 In a .... TV, a large box contains both the projector and the screen built in.
5 The gas mixture in a .... is not dangerous.

You and computers

Describe the 'home cinema' of your dreams. Use these notes to help you.

- ▪ Type of display: CRT television, LCD screen, plasma TV or video projector
- ▪ Screen size
- ▪ Resolution (image quality)
- ▪ Video source: TV, VCR or DVD recorder
- ▪ Sound capabilities

8 Processing

A The processor

The **processor**, also called the **CPU** or central processing unit, is the brain of your computer. In PCs, it is built into a single **chip** – a small piece of silicon with a complex electrical circuit, called an integrated circuit – that executes instructions and coordinates the activities of all the other units.

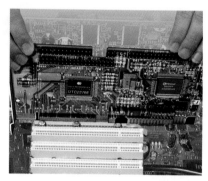

An Intel microprocessor chip, the nerve centre of many PCs

Three typical parts are:
- the **control unit,** which examines instructions from memory and executes them;
- the **arithmetic and logic unit** (**ALU**), which performs arithmetic and logical operations;
- the **registers**, high-speed units of memory used to store and control data.

The speed of a processor is measured in **gigahertz** (GHz). Thus, a CPU running at 4 GHz can make about four thousand million calculations a second. An internal **clock** sends out signals at fixed intervals to measure and synchronize the flow of data.

The main circuit board is known as the **motherboard**. This contains the CPU, the memory chips, expansion slots and controllers for peripherals, connected by internal **buses,** or paths, that carry electronic signals. For example, the **front side bus** carries all data that passes from the CPU to other devices.

Expansion slots allow you to install **expansion cards** which provide extra functions, e.g. a video card or a modem. Laptops have PC cards, the size of a credit card, which add features like sound, memory and network capabilities.

Fitting an expansion card

B RAM and ROM

When you run a program, the CPU looks for it on the hard disk and transfers a copy into the **RAM. RAM** (**random access memory**) is temporary or volatile, that is, it holds data while your PC is working on it, but loses this data when the power is switched off.

However, **ROM** (**read only memory**) is permanent and contains instructions needed by the CPU; the **BIOS** (basic input/output system) uses ROM to control communication with peripherals, e.g. disk drives.

The amount of RAM determines the number of programs you can run simultaneously and how fast they operate. It can be **expanded** by adding extra RAM chips.

A RAM module

C Units of memory

The electronic circuits in computers detect the difference between two states: ON (the current passes through) or OFF (the current doesn't); they represent these states as 1 or 0. Each 1 or 0 is called a **binary digit** or **bit**.

Bits are grouped into eight-digit codes that typically represent characters (letters, numbers and symbols). Eight bits together are called a **byte**. For example, 01000001 is used for the character A. Computers use a standard code called ASCII for the binary representation of characters.

One bit
01000001
Example of a byte

In order to avoid complex calculations of bytes, we use bigger units. A **kilobyte** (KB) is 1,024 bytes; a **megabyte** (MB) is 1,024 kilobytes; a **gigabyte** (GB) is 1,024 megabytes; a **terabyte** (TB) is 1,024 gigabytes. We use these units to describe the RAM memory, the operating capacity of disks and the size of a program or document.

8.1 Look at A and B opposite. Then match the sentence beginnings (1–6) with the correct endings (a–f).

1 The CPU processes data and   a areas within the CPU.
2 The control unit is the part of the CPU that   b you can't make changes to it.
3 The arithmetic and logic unit is able to make   c controls the way instructions are executed.
4 The registers are high-speed storage   d the computer is turned off.
5 Data contained in RAM is lost when   e coordinates the other parts of the computer.
6 ROM memory can only be read: f calculations: add, subtract, multiply and divide.

8.2 Solve the clues and complete the puzzle with words from the opposite page.

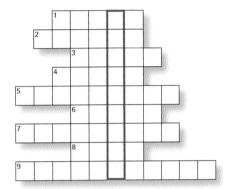

1 Intel .... are used in many computers.
2 Each 0 or 1 is called a bit, short for .... digit.
3 Special cards can be inserted into expansion ....
4 A .... controls the timing within the PC by sending signals to synchronize its circuits and operations.
5 The processor speed is measured in ....
6 .... carry signals between different parts of a PC.
7 .... cards improve the computer's performance.
8 The .... uses ROM to control the input/output of data.
9 The main printed circuit board is called the ....

Down: The brain of a computer

8.3 Read this product description and answer the questions below.

1 How fast is the CPU?
2 Which term is used to describe the CPU data bus?
3 How much RAM does the computer have?
4 Can you add extra RAM chips? How many?

Processor and memory:
• Intel Core 2 Duo processor at 2.4 GHz
• 533 MHz Front Side Bus
• 1,024 MB of RAM; can be expanded up to 4 GB
200 GB Hard disk
Double Layer DVD +/-R/RW drive
Microsoft Windows

8.4 Look at C opposite. Fill in the blanks with the correct unit of memory.

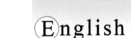

1 One .... represents one character.

2 One .... represents 1,024 characters (about a small page of text).

3 One .... represents about one million characters (about the text of a small book).

4 One .... represents about 1,000,000,000 characters (about 1,000 books).

5 One .... represents about 1,000,000,000,000 characters (about one million books in a big library).

You and computers

Access the *Professional English in Use ICT* website at www.cambridge.org/elt/ict. Then do the activity <u>Acronyms and abbreviations</u>.

9 Disks and drives

A Magnetic storage

Magnetic devices store data magnetically. A disk drive spins the disk at high speed and reads its data or writes new data onto it.

The inside of a hard disk drive

- **A floppy disk drive** uses 3.5 inch diskettes which can only hold 1.44 MB of data; it's often called A: drive and is relatively slow.

- Most PCs have one internal **hard disk**, usually called C: drive, which can hold several gigabytes of data. It's used to keep the operating system, the programs and the user's files easily available for use.

  When you **format a disk**, or prepare it for use, its surface is divided into concentric circles called **tracks**. Each track is further divided into a number of **sectors**. The computer remembers where information is stored by noting the track and sector numbers in a directory.

  The average time required for the read/write heads to move and find data is called **access time**; it is measured in milliseconds (ms). Don't confuse 'access time' with '**transfer rate**', the rate of transmission of data from the disk to the CPU (e.g. 15 megabytes per second).

sector   track

- A **portable hard drive** is an external unit with the drive mechanism and the media all in one sealed case. You can use it to **make a backup**, a spare copy of your files, or to transport data between computers.

B Optical storage

Optical drives use a laser to read and write data, so they are not affected by magnetic fields; but they are slower than hard drives. Modern DVD recorders accept all **CD** and **DVD** formats.

CDs (compact discs) can store up to 650–700 MB of data. • **CD-ROMs** (read only memory) are 'read-only' units, so you cannot change data stored on them (e.g. a dictionary or a game). • **CD-R** (recordable) discs are write-once devices which let you duplicate CDs. • **CD-RW** (rewritable) discs enable you to write onto them in multiple sessions, like a hard disk.	**DVDs** (digital versatile discs) are similar in size to CDs (both are 1.2 mm thick), but they differ in structure and capacity. DVDs have more tracks and more pits (tiny holes) per track, and can store from 4.7 GB to 17 GB of data, movies, high-definition sound, etc., so they will probably replace CDs. DVD formats include: • **DVD-ROM** (read-only memory) • **DVD-R** or **DVD+R** (recordable only once) • **DVD-RW** or **DVD+RW** (rewritable, so it can be erased and reused many times).

Portable DVD players let you watch movies or TV, play games and listen to music, wherever you are. They usually run on batteries, have a **widescreen** (rectangular 16:9 format) LCD and support **multi-format playback**, allowing you access to many file formats including DVD video, JPEG pictures, MP3 music, etc. They have two built-in stereo speakers, or **headphones** if you don't want to disturb other people.

C Removable flash memory

Flash memory is solid-state, rewritable memory; it is non-volatile, so it retains data when the power is turned off. This explains its popularity in small devices.

CompactFlash memory card

- **Flash memory cards** such as CompactFlash or Secure Digital are found in cameras, PDAs and music players.

- **Flash drives**, also known as thumb or pen drives, are connected to a USB port of the computer. They let you save and transfer data easily.

Mini flash drives

9.1 Read A opposite. Choose a term from this word web to complete the sentences below.

```
        hard disk      access time
                                      floppy disk drive
   transfer rate     Magnetic storage
                                      portable hard drive
        backup      sectors    tracks
```

1 The first rule of data storage is to make a .... of all important files.
2 A .... is slower than a hard drive and can only hold 1.44 MB disks.
3 The .... inside your PC is made of aluminium alloy covered with a magnetic coating. This makes the disk itself a rigid plate, hence its name.
4 The .... are circles around a disk and the .... are segments within each circle.
5 This hard drive is a 60 GB IBM model with a fast .... of 8 ms.
6 The .... is the rate of transmission of data from the disk to the CPU. This is usually described in megabytes per second.
7 Apple's iPod music player can double as a .... for transporting computer data.

9.2 Look at the opposite page and find:

1 the CD and DVD formats that can be rewritten many times
2 the CD and DVD formats that can be written to by the user only once
3 the CD and DVD formats that can be read by a computer but not written to
4 the type of cards used in digital cameras
5 a type of drive that plugs into a USB port and lets you share photos and music with friends
6 the memory without moving parts; it is erasable, non-volatile and used in small devices
7 the expression that means to 'initialize a disk and prepare it to receive data'

9.3 Complete this product description with words from B opposite.

The Panasonic DVD-LS91 is a top-of-the-range (1) .... , which provides pure entertainment wherever you go.

It has a big 9 inch built-in (2) .... LCD, so you can really enjoy movies. The built-in stereo speakers allow you to listen along, or if you want to listen alone, just plug in a pair of (3) .... This portable machine provides (4) ....-................................. .... , so you can play DVD Audio/Video, CD-R/RW, DVD-RAM, DivX and MP3 files. Its compact design features a built-in rechargeable 6 hour battery pack.

The DVD-LS91 allows 6 hours of playback, and provides a perfect way to entertain yourself and your kids during long trips.

Panasonic portable DVD player

You and computers

Which device or format would be most suitable for storing these things?

1 the operating system and the programs on a home computer
2 an electronic encyclopedia for children
3 a movie in digital format
4 the music tracks by your favourite artist
5 all the files generated by a company in one day
6 the photos taken with a digital camera

"I forgot to make a backup copy of my brain, so everything I learned last semester was lost."

10 | Health and safety

A | Computer ergonomics

There are a number of health and safety problems that may result from continuous use of computers.

- Typing constantly at high speed may provoke **repetitive strain injury** or **RSI**, which causes pain in the neck, arms, wrists, hands and fingers.
- Bad work postures and sitting in uncomfortable chairs may cause backache and stress.
- Looking at the screen for long periods of time, and lights reflecting off the screen, can cause headaches and **eye strain**, pain and fatigue of the eyes.
- Cathode Ray Tube monitors can emit electromagnetic radiation which can be dangerous to health.

The study of how people interact safely and efficiently with machines and their work conditions is called **ergonomics**. In computing, ergonomics is about designing computer facilities so they are safe and comfortable. Here are a few tips.

An ergonomic keyboard helps you type in a more natural, relaxed position

1. Get an **adjustable chair** so you can change its height and angle.
2. Make sure your **feet rest firmly** on the ground or on a foot rest.
3. Ensure you have **enough leg room** under the desk.
4. Put the **monitor at eye level** or just below.
5. Sit **at arms' length from the monitor** (40–80 cm). Don't sit near the sides or back of CRT monitors; or use LCD screens, which are free from radiation.
6. Use a **document holder**, in line with the screen, to reduce awkward neck and eye movements between the document and the screen.
7. Position the **keyboard at the same height as your elbows**, with your arms parallel to the work surface. Try to keep your **wrists straight** and flat when typing.
8. Take regular breaks from the computer and look away from the screen at regular intervals.

B | Electronic rubbish

Irresponsible disposal of **electronic waste**, from old computers and mobile phones to hi-fi and video systems, can cause severe environmental and public health problems. For example, children or workers who come into contact with the toxic components of electronic products may suffer from skin and breathing problems.

We should reduce, reuse and recycle e-waste

- We should **recycle** or treat ICT equipment (e.g. plastics from mobiles could be used to make pens and rulers).
- Manufacturers should pay to finance recycling programs.

C | The risks of using mobiles and in-car computers

Frequent use of mobile phones has been the cause of concern and there is ongoing research into whether radiation emitted causes health problems.

A serious risk is the **use of mobiles** and navigation systems in cars; this can distract the driver and cause accidents.

- Don't use your mobile while driving.

Another health problem is **Internet addiction**, including obsessive game playing, gambling, etc.

- If you are an Internet addict, you should ask for help from specialists.

Talking on a mobile phone when driving is illegal in most countries

10.1 Match the numbers in the picture to the correct tips in the checklist.

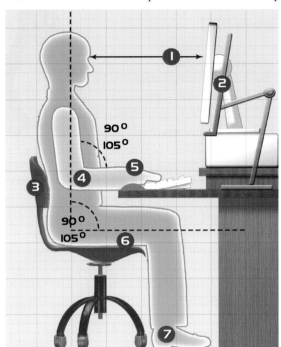

Tips for a user-friendly workstation

a Consistent chair support for the lower back. Seat height and angle adjustable.
b Feet flat on the floor.
c Document holder beside the screen, at the same height and distance as the screen.
d Text on the screen in line with the eyes. Viewing distance at arm's length.
e Thighs horizontal, with feet on the floor. Adequate room for legs beneath the desk.
f Keyboard height at a comfortable open angle for the elbows and arms.
g Wrists and hands in a neutral position, in line with the forearms. Optional rest for wrists at the same height as the keyboard.

10.2 Complete the sentences with words from the opposite page.

1 Experts believe the best way to reduce musculoskeletal injuries is through ....
– designing jobs to fit people instead of making people fit the job. It can mean everything from adjusting the height of a desk to buying a new chair or overhauling a production line.
2 The Safetype ergonomic keyboard may look strange, but its makers claim that it can prevent .... or RSI.
3 Visual problems, such as .... and irritation, are often reported by computer users. Causes of these problems include glare, poor lighting, and focusing the eyes on the screen for a prolonged period.
4 Some companies have begun to test ways to .... and dispose of ....
.... For example, Epson Portland sponsored an electronics collection day this year on Earth Day.
5 Road safety campaigners say motorists using .... while driving are six times more likely to crash.
6 When a person is spending so much time on the Internet that their lives are affected negatively, they are suffering from ....

You and computers

Imagine you are designing an ICT classroom with 16 networked PCs, Internet access and peripherals. What safety precautions should be taken into account? Use these notes to help you write four tips or suggestions.

1 Room conditions (space, desks, chairs, lights and windows)

2 Ergonomic devices

3 Electrical safety: layout of cables and connectors, hotspots for a wireless network, etc.

4 Noticeboards and posters with health and safety recommendations

11 Operating systems and the GUI

A Types of software; the operating system (OS)

1 **System software** controls the basic functions of a computer, e.g. operating systems, programming software and utility programs.
2 **Application software** lets you do specific jobs such as writing letters, doing calculations, drawing or playing games. Examples are a word processor or a graphics package.

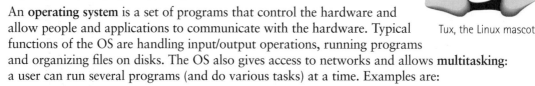

Tux, the Linux mascot

An **operating system** is a set of programs that control the hardware and allow people and applications to communicate with the hardware. Typical functions of the OS are handling input/output operations, running programs and organizing files on disks. The OS also gives access to networks and allows **multitasking**: a user can run several programs (and do various tasks) at a time. Examples are:

■ the **Windows** family – designed by Microsoft and used on most PCs
■ **Mac OS** – created by Apple and used on Macintosh computers
■ **Unix** – found on mainframes and workstations in corporate installations, as it supports multi-users
■ **Linux** – developed under the GNU General Public License; anyone can copy its source code, modify and redistribute it. It is used on PCs and in appliances and small devices.

B The Graphical User Interface

A **GUI** makes use of a **WIMP** environment: Windows, Icons, Menus and Pointer. This type of interface is **user-friendly**, where system functions are accessed by selecting self-explanatory **icons** (pictures representing **programs** or **documents**) and items from menus. A **drop-down menu**, or **pull-down menu**, is a list of options that appear below a menu bar when you click on an item.

The **pointer** is the arrow, controlled by the mouse, which lets you choose options from menus.

The background screen that displays icons, representing programs, files and **folders** (directories) is called the **desktop**. Double-clicking a folder icon opens a **window** which shows the programs, documents and other folders contained within the folder.

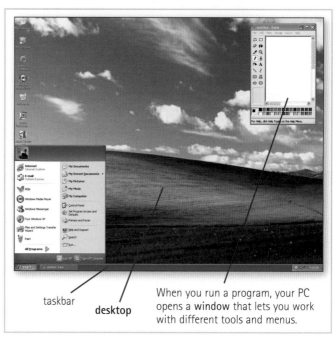

taskbar

desktop

When you run a program, your PC opens a **window** that lets you work with different tools and menus.

The Windows environment is a typical example of a GUI

C System utilities

These are small programs included with an OS that improve a system's performance. They can be desk accessories, device drivers, or system extensions activated when you turn on the PC.

■ A **crashed disk rescuer** is used to restore disks and corrupted files.
■ An **accessibility program** makes a PC easier for disabled users to use.
■ A **compression utility** rewrites data so that it takes less space on disk.
■ A **media player** lets you watch DVDs, play music and listen to the radio on the Web.

11.1 Read A and B opposite and find the following.

1 the difference between system software and application software
2 software that enables users and programs to communicate with hardware
3 the meaning of 'multitasking'
4 a multi-user OS used on large, powerful computer systems
5 the operating system that is freely distributed
6 the operating system designed by Apple
7 the OS created by Microsoft
8 the meaning of WIMP in a graphical user interface (GUI)
9 the expression used to describe a system that is easy to use

11.2 Look at B opposite and then identify these interface elements.

desktop	window	drop-down menu
pointer	folder	program icon
document icon		

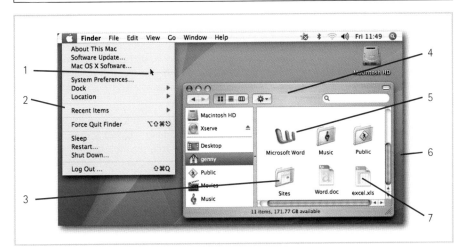

Apple Macintosh programs use a graphical user interface

11.3 Look at C opposite. Which utility would you use to do these tasks?

1 to play and organize multimedia on your PC
2 to diagnose and repair damaged disks
3 to help computer users with sight, hearing or mobility difficulties
4 to make files smaller, so you can send them with emails

"Susan! ... Are you trying to tell me we have an interface problem?"

You and computers

1 Write a sentence explaining why Windows is so popular.

2 Look at the Internet and find two operating systems designed for hand-held devices such as PDAs, palmtops and Blackberries.

12 Word processing features

A

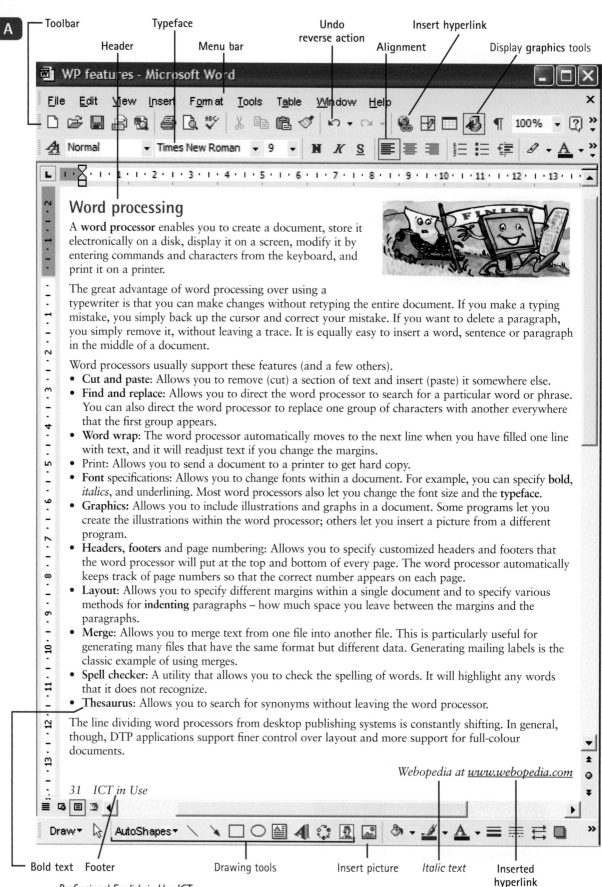

Toolbar · Header · Typeface · Menu bar · Undo reverse action · Alignment · Insert hyperlink · Display graphics tools

Word processing

A **word processor** enables you to create a document, store it electronically on a disk, display it on a screen, modify it by entering commands and characters from the keyboard, and print it on a printer.

The great advantage of word processing over using a typewriter is that you can make changes without retyping the entire document. If you make a typing mistake, you simply back up the cursor and correct your mistake. If you want to delete a paragraph, you simply remove it, without leaving a trace. It is equally easy to insert a word, sentence or paragraph in the middle of a document.

Word processors usually support these features (and a few others).

- **Cut and paste:** Allows you to remove (cut) a section of text and insert (paste) it somewhere else.
- **Find and replace:** Allows you to direct the word processor to search for a particular word or phrase. You can also direct the word processor to replace one group of characters with another everywhere that the first group appears.
- **Word wrap:** The word processor automatically moves to the next line when you have filled one line with text, and it will readjust text if you change the margins.
- Print: Allows you to send a document to a printer to get hard copy.
- **Font** specifications: Allows you to change fonts within a document. For example, you can specify **bold**, *italics*, and underlining. Most word processors also let you change the font size and the **typeface**.
- **Graphics:** Allows you to include illustrations and graphs in a document. Some programs let you create the illustrations within the word processor; others let you insert a picture from a different program.
- **Headers, footers** and page numbering: Allows you to specify customized headers and footers that the word processor will put at the top and bottom of every page. The word processor automatically keeps track of page numbers so that the correct number appears on each page.
- **Layout:** Allows you to specify different margins within a single document and to specify various methods for **indenting** paragraphs – how much space you leave between the margins and the paragraphs.
- **Merge:** Allows you to merge text from one file into another file. This is particularly useful for generating many files that have the same format but different data. Generating mailing labels is the classic example of using merges.
- **Spell checker:** A utility that allows you to check the spelling of words. It will highlight any words that it does not recognize.
- **Thesaurus:** Allows you to search for synonyms without leaving the word processor.

The line dividing word processors from desktop publishing systems is constantly shifting. In general, though, DTP applications support finer control over layout and more support for full-colour documents.

Webopedia at www.webopedia.com

31   ICT in Use

Bold text · Footer · Drawing tools · Insert picture · *Italic text* · Inserted hyperlink

12.1 Match words from the opposite page with these definitions.

1 a program used for preparing documents and letters
2 a row of words that open up menus when selected
3 the distinctive design of letters and characters, e.g. **Arial**, `Courier`
4 text printed in the top margin
5 text printed in the bottom margin
6 the way text is arranged on the page, including margins, paragraph format, columns, etc.
7 a function that enables you to combine two files into one

12.2 Label these word processing icons with the correct function.

a cut and paste   b graphics   c align left   d undo   e insert hyperlink

1 ....   2 ....   3 ....   4 ....   5 ....

12.3 Complete these statements with a term from A opposite.

1 A .... consists of three elements: typeface, type style and type size; for example **Arial bold at 9 points**.
2 Notice that when you get to the end of each line, Word starts a new line automatically. It moves the word you are typing to a new line when it enters an invisible margin running down the right-hand side of the screen. This feature is called ....
3 .... and .... lets you find a word and change it into another word throughout the text.
4 A good .... program can be used not only to rectify accidental spelling mistakes and typing errors, but also to speed typing input.
5 Many word processors include a ...., so you can look for words with similar meanings.
6 The .... contains a row of icons that perform particular actions when clicked.
7 .... a paragraph involves moving your writing in from the margins of the page. For example, a left indent is the distance between the left margin and the text.

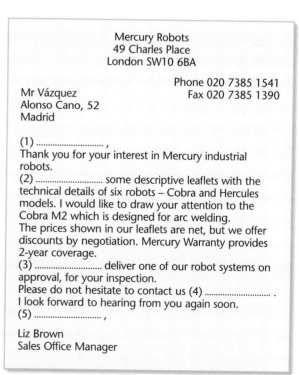

You and computers

Type the letter or copy it from the website to your word processor. Then edit it by making these changes.

1 Use Times New Roman at 10 points.
2 Insert these phrases in the correct places:
   a Yours sincerely
   b if you require any further information
   c Please find enclosed
   d Dear Mr Vázquez
   f We would be pleased to
3 Align the sender's address to the right.
4 Insert this email address below the fax number: mercury@tinyworld.co.uk
5 Change Cobra M2 to italic style and Mercury Warranty to bold style.
6 Insert a company logo and a picture of a robot; you can download them from the Web.
7 Check the spelling.

Mercury Robots
49 Charles Place
London SW10 6BA

Phone 020 7385 1541
Fax 020 7385 1390

Mr Vázquez
Alonso Cano, 52
Madrid

(1) .... ,
Thank you for your interest in Mercury industrial robots.
(2) .... some descriptive leaflets with the technical details of six robots – Cobra and Hercules models. I would like to draw your attention to the Cobra M2 which is designed for arc welding.
The prices shown in our leaflets are net, but we offer discounts by negotiation. Mercury Warranty provides 2-year coverage.
(3) .... deliver one of our robot systems on approval, for your inspection.
Please do not hesitate to contact us (4) ....
I look forward to hearing from you again soon.
(5) .... ,

Liz Brown
Sales Office Manager

13 Spreadsheets and databases

A Spreadsheet basics

A **spreadsheet** program helps you manage personal and business finances. Spreadsheets, or worksheets, are mathematical tables which show figures in **rows** and **columns**.

A **cell** can hold three types of data: text, numbers and formulae.

Formulae are entries that have an equation which calculates the value to display; we can use them to calculate totals, percentages, discounts, etc.

Spreadsheets have many built-in **functions**, pre-written instructions that can be carried out by referring to the function by name. For example, =SUM(D2:D7) means add up all the values in the cell range D2 to D7.

The format menu lets you choose font, alignment, borders, etc.

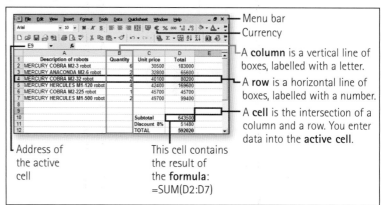

Address of the active cell

This cell contains the result of the formula: =SUM(D2:D7)

Menu bar

Currency

A **column** is a vertical line of boxes, labelled with a letter.

A **row** is a horizontal line of boxes, labelled with a number.

A **cell** is the intersection of a column and a row. You enter data into the **active cell**.

B Parts of a database

Database basics

A **database** is essentially a computerized record-keeping system.

Each unit of information you create is called a **record** and each record is made up of a collection of **fields**. Typically, a single record consists of a set of field names like: Title, FirstName, Surname, JobTitle, TelNo and ID. You fill in a form with the relevant information for each field to add a new record to the database. There are different **data types**.

A database file stores information in **fields** grouped on **records**

- **Text** – holds letters and numbers not used in calculations
- **Number** – can only hold numbers used in calculations and reports
- **Memo** – can store long texts
- **Date/Time** – a date or time or combination of both
- **AutoNumber** – assigns a number to each record
- **OLE Object** – (object linking and embedding) holds sounds and pictures
- **Yes/No** – for alternative values like true/false, yes/no, on/off, etc.
- **Hyperlink** – adds a link to a website

Once you have added data to a set of records, **indexes** must be created to help the database find specific records and **sort** (classify) records faster. An **index** performs the same function as in the back of a book or in a library. For example, if you regularly search your database by surname, the index should be defined on this field.

Relational databases

Two database files can be **related** or joined as long as they hold a piece of data in common. A file of employee names, for example, could include a field called 'DEPARTMENT NUMBER' and another file, containing details of the department itself, could include the same field. This common **field** can then be used to link the two files together.

Extracting information from a database is known as performing a **query**. For example, if you want to know all customers that spend more than £9,000 per month, the program will search the name field and the money field simultaneously.

13.1 Look at A opposite and find the terms which correspond with these definitions.

1 software which allows data to be displayed and managed in a table format
2 it goes up and down and has letter labels
3 it goes across and has number labels
4 an area in a spreadsheet which contains data
5 the current cell where you enter information
6 mathematical equations that help you calculate and analyze data
7 ready-to-use formulae that help you perform specialized calculations, e.g. SUM, AVERAGE, etc.

13.2 Study the tables and then complete the text below with words from B opposite.

⊞ **Students: Table**

ID	Name	Surname	Address	Teacher ID
1	Lucy	Reeve	3 Pond Road	106
2	Joe	Davey	7 Oxbury Close	107
3	Adam	Moore	4 Quebec Street	108

⊞ **Teachers: Table**

Teacher ID	Name	Surname	Address	Subject
106	James	Pullin	9 The Green	Maths
107	Liz	White	5 London Road	English
108	Karen	Southwell	8 Granary Street	ICT

Relationship between tables: the key field
has the same value in both tables

A (1) .... program allows the user to store, change and retrieve information.
A database file is a collection of records. Each (2) .... contains a set of fields.
Each (3) .... holds a separate piece of information; for example, a student file
contains a list of records, each of which consists of several fields which give their name,
address, birthday, etc.
In a (4) .... database, information is stored in tables that have a connection or
link with one another (see tables above).
A database lets you create an (5) ...., a list of records ordered according to
the content of certain fields; this helps you search and (6) .... records into
numerical or alphabetical order very fast. It also has a (7) .... function which
allows you to extract information that meets certain criteria.

13.3 Look at this form of a music
collection. Label the data types
with words from B opposite.

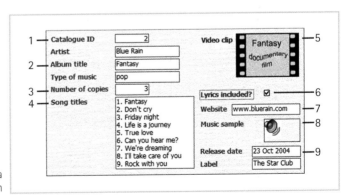

Form designed with Microsoft Access, a
typical database program

You and computers

Which data fields would you include in these databases?

1 the patients of a hospital

2 a library catalogue

14 Graphics and design

A Types of graphics software

Computer graphics are pictures created, changed or processed by computers. There are two categories.

1 **Bitmapped graphics** represent images as **bitmaps**; they are stored as pixels and can become a bit distorted when they are manipulated. The density of dots, known as the resolution and expressed in dots per inch, determines how sharp the image is.

2 **Vector graphics** represent images as mathematical formulae, so they can be changed or scaled without losing quality. They are ideal for high-resolution output.

There are different types of graphics software.

■ **Image manipulation programs** let you edit your favourite images. For example, you can scan a picture into your PC or transfer a photo from your camera and then add different effects, or **filters**.

■ **Painting and drawing programs**, also called **illustration packages**, offer facilities for freehand drawing, with a wide choice of pens and brushes, colours and patterns. One example is *Windows Paint*.

■ **Business graphics programs**, also called **presentation software**, let you create pie charts, bar charts and line graphs of all kinds for slide shows and reports. You can import data from a database or spreadsheet to generate the graphs.

■ **Computer-aided design (CAD)** is used by engineers and architects to design everything from cars and planes to buildings and furniture. First they make a **wireframe**, a drawing with edges and contour lines. Then if they want to colour the objects and add texture, they create a surface for the object; this is called 'filling the surface'. Finally, the design is **rendered** to make the object look realistic. **Rendering** is a process that adds realism to graphics by using shading, light sources and reflections.

■ **Desktop publishing (DTP)** is based around a page layout program, which lets you import text from a word processor, **clip-art** (ready-made pictures) from graphics packages, and images from scanners or cameras, and arrange them all on a page. It is used to design and publish books, newspapers, posters, advertisements, etc.

■ **Digital art**, or **computer art**, is done with applets that use mathematical formulae to create beautiful bright shapes called fractals. A **fractal** is a geometrical figure with special properties, e.g. the Koch snowflake or the Mandelbrot set. Fractals can also be used to model real objects like clouds, coastlines or landscapes.

■ **Computer animation** uses graphics programs (e.g. digital cartooning systems) to create or edit moving pictures. Each image in a sequence of images is called a 'frame'.

■ **Geographic information systems (GIS)** allow cartographers to create detailed maps.

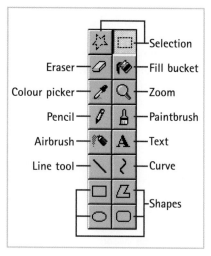

Windows Paint Toolbox

The original photo has been processed with Adobe Photoshop using effects **filters**

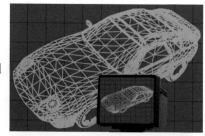

3D wireframe drawing

14.1 Read A opposite and decide which type of graphics software is best for these users.

1 a person who wants to edit photos at home
2 an economist who wants to present statistics in a form that can be easily understood
3 engineers who need to design the interior and exterior of a new aeroplane
4 a company which needs to design and publish a magazine
5 an artist who wants to produce illustrations and freehand drawings for a book
6 an organization that needs to make maps and 3D virtual models of the surface of the Earth
7 computer animators who make movies like *Toy Story* and *Shrek*
8 a mathematician who wants to make fractal shapes of natural phenomena

14.2 Complete the sentences with words from the box.

wireframe	bitmap	fractals
rendering	filters	clip-art

1 Painting programs work by giving a colour to each pixel in an image, creating a .... Unlike vector graphics, the image is a single layer, so once something is painted, it becomes part of the whole picture.
2 In painting programs and image editors, ... are special effects that can be applied to a picture, including drop shadows, textures, distortions, etc.
3 The .... model is the simplest interpretation of a true three-dimensional object. Here the object is represented by its edges and contours and is therefore similar in form to a normal engineering drawing or sketch.
4 .... adds textures to each surface, and generates realistic reflections, shadows and highlights.
5 Most illustration packages come with a bundle of resources that include ready-made .... images and a selection of fonts.
6 .... are geometrical patterns that are repeated at a small scale to generate irregular shapes, some of which are similar to objects in nature.

Example of a fractal

14.3 Look at the *Windows Paint* toolbox opposite and find the tools that match these definitions.

1 This is like a magnifying glass which changes your view of a drawing.
2 This brush lets you paint in different shapes and patterns.
3 This is used to draw curves in different thicknesses.
4 This rubs out the part of the picture you drag it over.
5 This tool lets you pick a colour from an area of an image, instead of choosing the colour from the colour palette.
6 This tool is used to fill a shape with a colour of your choice.
7 This makes straight lines.
8 This basic tool is used to draw freehand, i.e. to draw free-form shapes.
9 This group of tools is used for drawing shapes: rectangles, ellipses and polygons.
10 This produces individual pixels of colour in a spray pattern.
11 These tools let you make rectangular or freehand selections around the things you want to select.
12 This is used to type text.

You and computers

1 Write about two possible applications of using computer graphics in business.

2 Can you think of one advantage of using computer graphics in the car industry?

3 You probably have a paint program at home; describe what you do with it.

15 Multimedia

A A multimedia system

Multimedia refers to the technologies and applications that integrate different media: text, graphics, sound, video and animation.

Its power resides in interactivity, hypertext and hypermedia. Multimedia software is usually **interactive**, so you can choose what you want to watch, listen to or write. **Hypertext** means that you can click on a word and jump to another screen with more information; **hypermedia** is similar, but works with sounds and images (e.g. the Web).

An IT student says:

> 'I use multimedia for my extracurricular activities. I download music from the Net and **burn music** onto CDs – I copy songs onto CDs. I talk with my friends on the Messenger. I also retouch digital pictures and edit video clips.
> To run multimedia software you need a fast CPU, expandable RAM and a large hard disk. But what marks a computer out as a **multimedia** PC is its audio and video capabilities: a sound card, a microphone, a decent pair of speakers, a high-quality monitor and a DVD writer; and its performance depends on all these components working in harmony.'

B Recognizing file formats

To identify the type of file, an **extension** is added to the filename when it is saved on disk.

 Common text extensions:
.pdf (portable document format)
.doc (*MS Word* document)
.rtf (rich text format)
.htm or **.html** (hypertext markup language for Web files)

 Graphics include charts, photos, drawings, buttons, etc.
.gif (graphics interchange format)
.jpg (jpeg – joint photographic experts group)
.tif (tagged image file)

 You can hear sound such as songs, movie soundtracks and speeches. Common **audio** formats:
.wav (*Windows* wave audio format)
.ra (*RealAudio* file)
.mp3 (compressed music files)

 Video refers to recording, editing and displaying moving images. Common formats:
.avi (audio video interleave)
.mov (*QuickTime* movie)
.mpg (**mpeg** – moving picture experts group)

 Animations are made up of a series of independent pictures put together in sequence to look like moving pictures. Common formats:
.gif for animated gifs
.swf for *Flash* files

 Files **compressed** with *Winzip* have a .zip extension.
A popular format used to compress and distribute movies on DVDs or over the Net is **DivX**, a digital video codec (COmpress, DECompress).

C Applications

- In public places (e.g. museums and stations), there are information kiosks that use multimedia.

- In education, it is used in presentations and computer-based training courses.

- On the Web, audio and video are integrated into web pages. For example, RealPlayer supports **streaming**, which lets you play sound (e.g. from radio stations) and video files as a continuous stream while they are downloading.

- In **virtual reality,** users interact with a simulated world: doctors train using virtual surgery; pilots use flight simulators to do their training; people visit virtual exhibitions, etc.

- You can play games on a computer or **video games** on a dedicated machine, called a **video console,** which you connect to a TV set. You can also play games on the Net; some websites have a **multiplayer** facility that enables lots of people to play the same game at the same time.

Multimedia has had a profound impact on encyclopedias

15.1 Look at A and B opposite and find the following.

1 the type of text that contains links to other texts
2 the expression that means 'to record music onto a CD'
3 a system that combines hypertext and multimedia
4 the most common extensions for graphics files
5 the most common text formats
6 three popular video formats
7 three common file formats for storing audio data

15.2 Solve the clues and complete the puzzle with words from the opposite page.

1 A series of still images shown in sequence.
2 .... files are processed by sound software.
3 In medicine, doctors use virtual .... systems to simulate particular situations.
4 The suffix placed after a dot at the end of a filename.
5 A format used to compress and transmit movies over the Web.
6 People use special programs to .... and decompress files so that they occupy less disk space.
7 A video format developed by the Moving Picture Experts Group.
8 A system of filming, processing and showing moving pictures.
9 .gif stands for .... interchange format.
10 The technique which allows you to play music and watch video before the entire file has downloaded.

Down: The combination of moving and still images, sound, music and words.

15.3 Complete the article with the words from the box.

graphics	interactive	video games	consoles	multiplayer

Video Games

There are games you play on video (1) .... such as Nintendo, Sega, and the PlayStation. And there are games you play on a computer, either alone or at multiplayer online sites such as Microsoft's Internet Gaming Zone and Battle.net.
(2) .... have been made into films, such as *Mortal Kombat 1* and *2*, and film stars now sometimes appear in video games. The (3) .... in many games have taken on such a high degree of realism that they almost seem like film. The *X-Files* game was practically an (4) .... movie, full of actors from the show and sections of dialogue and video. Some people claim that the *Blade Runner* video game was better than the movie – not only were the sets incredible but you also got to control the action and the ending.
(5) .... online gaming is the next wave in the video game world. It provides a better gaming experience, simply because people are more creative and more challenging adversaries than computers. Thousands of people can play simultaneously all over the world.   *Video Games*

You and computers

1 Have you ever used a multimedia encyclopedia? If so, note down three important features about it.

2 Write one advantage of using multimedia in a presentation.

3 Do you like video and computer games? Make a list of pros and cons.

16 Sound and music

Audio files on the Web

> I can listen to real-world or online radio stations with **Internet radio** everywhere in the world.

> I've just started a new **audioblog**. It's a blog, an Internet journal, which includes audio clips.

> I enjoy **podcasting**: I publish my own radio programmes as **podcasts**, audio files which I make available over the Internet for playback on people's computers. Also, I subscribe to other people's podcasts so that I can hear their radio programmes.

> My son downloads and listens to MP3 files he finds on **fileshare sites**, where you search and download music from other people's computers using software such as Kazaa or eMule.

> I ask my students to listen to **audio books** and get information from **audio lectures** and **spoken tutorials** on the Web.

All the people above describe different types of **webcasts,** broadcasts on the Web. These require either suitable audio player software (e.g. WinAmp or iTunes) that allows **streaming** a technique that means you can listen to an audio file while it's being downloaded; or a **plug-in** (e.g. RealPlayer or Windows Media Player), a program that interacts with your web browser to play audio files through the browser interface.

B ## Digital audio players

An iPod Nano enables you to store lots of music in a very small device

The different types of digital audio players are often referred to as **MP3 players. MP3** is short for **MPEG audio layer 3,** a type of compression used to reduce large files, such as songs, to manageable sizes. They come in different formats. Broadly speaking, **hard drive** versions, which include **iPods,** store greater amounts of music. **Built-in** or **flash memory,** which is more common in mini-MP3 players, holds fewer songs, but as there are no moving parts there are no problems with skipping. You have to upload the music from a CD onto a computer, **rip** a CD, or else download it from the Internet and then transfer it to the player.

With a suitable **ID3 editor** or jukebox program you can create **ID3 tags,** a set of data added to MP3 files, to organize your MP3 collection with information about the artists, albums, songs, etc.

C ## Other audio applications

1 Music can be composed, mixed, recorded and played back using **MIDI, musical instrument digital interface,** a standard protocol that enables computers and synthesizers to communicate with each other exchanging musical information. **DAWs, digital audio workstations,** record, edit and play back digital music.
2 The human voice can be decoded by a computer with suitable **speech recognition** software, allowing continuous speech dictation. This technology also enables spoken commands to control the computer.
3 Computers can produce sounds similar to a human voice with **speech synthesis** technologies, also called **text-to-speech** systems.

DAWs enable the creation of digital music

16.1 Solve the clues and complete the puzzle with words from A opposite.

Across
1 Auxiliary programs used to play multimedia files.
2 Students may be interested in this type of book and lecture.
6 The type of site where you can find and exchange music files.
7 An online journal with sound.

Down
1 The technology needed to publish radio programmes on the Web.
3 A podcast and a spoken tutorial are different types of ....
4 This technique allows you to listen to live online radio programmes.
5 .... radio includes both traditional and online radio stations.

16.2 Complete this text about digital audio players with words from B opposite.

Before buying your digital audio player, or [1] .... as they are usually known, you should take certain things into account.

First, size. Most [2] .... models tend to be bigger and heavier. On the other hand, if you buy a lighter version with flash [3] .... you won't be able to store so many songs, but the batteries will last longer and you'll be able to take it on your morning run as there won't be any problems with skipping.

[4] .... used to come in hard drive versions only, but the latest Nano model has [5] .... memory.

Whatever you choose, you'll have to download the music files from the Web or [6] .... your CDs and then compress the songs into the [7] .... format.

Finally, to make your playlists it's a good idea to install an [8] .... editor program that creates [9] .... with the name of the song, artist, etc.

16.3 Which audio application in C opposite are these people interested in?

1 I was fed up with typing long documents or dictating them to someone else. Now I just have to speak to my computer.
2 I enjoy manipulating the sounds I create with a synthesizer.
3 I'm a teacher in a school for the visually impaired. My pupils find this new technology very helpful.
4 I need this device to create digital music.

You and computers

Access the *Professional English in Use ICT* website at www.cambridge.org/elt/ict. Then do the activity <u>Create your own podcast</u>.

17 Programming

A Programming languages

Programming is the process of writing a program using a computer language. A **program** is a set of instructions which a computer uses to do a specific task (e.g. a solution to a Maths problem).

The only language a PC can directly execute is **machine code**, which consists of 1s and 0s. This language is difficult to write, so we use symbolic languages that are easier to understand. For example, **assembly languages** use abbreviations such as ADD, SUB, MPY to represent instructions. The program is then translated into machine code by software called an **assembler**.

Machine code and assembly languages are called low-level languages because they are closer to the hardware.

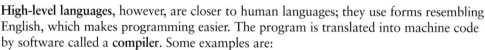

High-level languages, however, are closer to human languages; they use forms resembling English, which makes programming easier. The program is translated into machine code by software called a **compiler**. Some examples are:

- FORTRAN – used for scientific and mathematical applications
- COBOL – popular for business applications
- BASIC – used as a teaching language; Visual BASIC is now used to create Windows applications
- C – used to write system software, graphics and commercial programs
- Java – designed to run on the Web; **Java applets** are small programs that run automatically on web pages and let you watch animated characters, and play music and games.

The languages used to create Web documents are called **markup languages**; they use instructions (markups) to format and link text files. Examples are:

- **HTML** – the code used to create Web pages
- **VoiceXML** – it makes Internet content accessible via **speech recognition** and phone. Instead of using a web browser on a PC, you use a telephone to access voice-equipped websites. You just **dial** the phone number of the website and then give spoken instructions, **commands**, and get the required information.

B Steps in writing a program

To write a program, software developers usually follow these steps.

- First they try to understand the problem and define the purpose of the program.
- They design a **flowchart**, a diagram which shows the successive logical steps of the program.
- Next they write the instructions in a high-level language (Pascal, C, etc.). This is called **coding**. The program is then **compiled**.
- When the program is written, they **test** it: they run the program to see if it works and use special tools to detect **bugs**, or errors. Any errors are corrected until it runs smoothly. This is called **debugging**, or bug fixing.
- Finally, software companies write a detailed description of how the program works, called **program documentation**. They also have a **maintenance** program. They get reports from users about any errors found in the program. After it has been improved, it is published as an updated version.

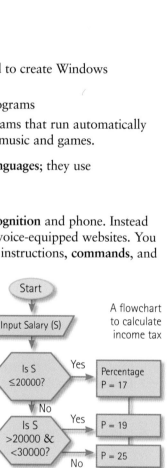

A flowchart to calculate income tax

17.1 Match the terms from A opposite with their definitions.

1 programming	a	basic language which consists of binary codes
2 machine code	b	programming language such as C, Java or Visual BASIC
3 assembly language	c	writing computer programs
4 high-level language	d	low-level language translated into machine code by an assembler
5 Java applet	e	software which converts a source program into machine code
6 compiler	f	language used to create and format documents for the Web
7 markup language	g	small self-contained program written in Java

17.2 Look at B and then put these programming steps into the correct order.

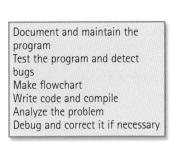
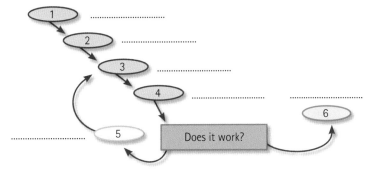

Document and maintain the program
Test the program and detect bugs
Make flowchart
Write code and compile
Analyze the problem
Debug and correct it if necessary

Does it work?

17.3 Complete this article about the *VoiceXML* application language with the words from the box.

HTML	dial	VoiceXML	commands	speech recognition

Internet: Voice recognition takes off

You don't need a sophisticated cell phone to surf the Internet when you're on the road – just your own voice. That's the idea behind a new breed of voice service that is popping up all over the place. Subscribers (1) .... a toll-free phone number and use spoken (2) .... to listen to anything from weather conditions to stock quotes, or flight information to news stories. Half a dozen of these services – such as Audiopoint, BeVocal, TellMe and TelSurf Networks – have already gone live or are testing their systems.

These launches are all happening because two crucial technologies have come of age. (3) .... software from companies such as Lucent, Nuance and Speechworks can now understand a wide range of accents and diction without having to be trained to a specific voice. And computer languages such as VoiceXML make it as easy to write voice services as (4) .... has made it to write web pages. With (5) .... , the human voice becomes a substitute for a computer mouse and the spoken command for a click. It doesn't, however, call up conventional web pages, but content which is specially composed for a telephone: sound clips, numbers, music, spoken texts.

The Economist

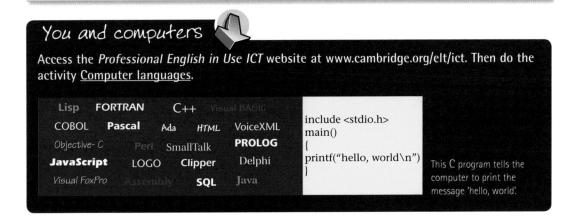

You and computers

Access the *Professional English in Use ICT* website at www.cambridge.org/elt/ict. Then do the activity Computer languages.

Lisp   FORTRAN   C++   Visual BASIC
COBOL   Pascal   Ada   HTML   VoiceXML
Objective-C   Perl   SmallTalk   PROLOG
JavaScript   LOGO   Clipper   Delphi
Visual FoxPro   Assembly   SQL   Java

```
include <stdio.h>
main()
{
printf("hello, world\n")
}
```

This C program tells the computer to print the message 'hello, world'.

18 Computers and work

A Jobs in computing

Most ICT-related jobs have developed to meet the need to analyze, design, develop, manage or support computer software, hardware or networks.

All the people involved in the different stages of development of a computer project, i.e. analysts, programmers, support specialists, etc. are controlled by a **project manager**.

> ### ANALYZE
> A **database analyst** is in charge of the research and development of databases; **network analysts** study the network requirements and recommend the most suitable type of network; **systems analysts** decide what ICT system will cater for the requirements of a specific institution.
>
> ### DESIGN AND DEVELOP
> **Web designers**, also called **webmasters**, create and maintain web pages and web applications for websites.
> **Software engineers**, either application programmers or systems programmers, plan, design, and test computer programs.
> **Hardware engineers** design and develop ICT devices.
> **Security specialists** specialize in the design of software and hardware to protect information from malware: viruses, spyware, etc.
>
> ### MANAGE
> **Network** or **computer systems administrators** install and maintain networks.
> **Database administrators** manage the accuracy and efficiency of databases.
>
> ### SUPPORT
> **Computer operators** control computer data processing.
> **Help desk technicians** are in charge of troubleshooting, the solution of technical problems.
> **Computer training instructors** or **trainers** teach people how to use hardware and software.
> **Technical writers** write the instructions for ICT systems.

A computer operator is in charge of computer data input and processing

B Computers and jobs: new ways, new profiles

With the development of ICT, there has been a change in the way lots of jobs are done.

> I've become a **teleworker**, a person who can work at home, thanks to **teleworking** or **telecommuting**, so I can work away from my official workplace. High-speed communications have made it possible.

> I'm training to work as an **online teacher**. I want to be a specialist in e-learning, distance education via the Internet.

> I started my career as a typesetter. Now I work as a **desktop publisher**: I create documents with DTP software.

> I like this new aspect of my job: I practise **telemedicine** - it's like having a long-distance surgery. Real-time data transmissions and virtual operations enable me to cure people who are far away.

> ICT has made my job much better and easier. Now I like to call myself a **computer animator**: with my computer I create cartoons I couldn't think of before.

18.1 Classify these jobs under the heading that best describes their function. They all appear in A opposite.

software engineer	help desk technician	database administrator
trainer	network analyst	systems analyst
hardware engineer	network administrator	

| ANALYZE | DESIGN/DEVELOP | MANAGE | SUPPORT |

a .... b .... c .... d .... e .... f .... g .... h ....

18.2 Draw lines between the columns to make true sentences about jobs in A opposite.

A technical	designer	controls all the operations and people in a project.
A project	writer	writes documentation of a program or device.
A web	specialist	plans and keeps websites updated.
A security	manager	designs applications against viruses.

18.3 What jobs in A opposite are being offered in these advertisements?

We are seeking a person to operate peripheral computer equipment, and perform report distribution duties and backup procedures on our servers.

Major Responsibilities
- Operating printers and unloading reports from the printer and distributing them through the internal mail system
- Performing backups on various operating systems
- Analysing and troubleshooting problems in the Data Centre reported by Help Desks or IT support associates

The successful candidate will be responsible for maintaining logical and physical database models as well as managing the database.

Job Requirements
- Bachelor's degree in Computer Science, a related field or equivalent experience
- Analytical skills and a proficiency in developing structured logic

18.4 Complete the text with words from B opposite.

The use of ICT has caused the development of new ways of working. People no longer need to be stuck in an office. Laptops, the Internet and wireless technologies allow (1) .... What's more, there are more and more people who have decided to become (2) .... and so have no need to travel to work at all.
The Internet has also enabled doctors to practise (3) .... and educators to work as (4) .... ICT technologies have introduced changes in the artistic world, too. Cartoons are now made by (5) .... and (6) ....
produce materials ready for publication.

You and computers

1 How have computers changed the way you work or study?

2 Make a list of the advantages and disadvantages that teleworking might have for you.

19 ICT systems

A ICT systems: components and functions

ICT systems are much more than computers. An **ICT system** involves the use of computers or other types of hardware to meet a specific need. A LAN, local area network, can be an example of an ICT system, but interactive television and the database of a library are types of systems too.

ICT systems have these components:
- **software,** instructions and data
- **hardware,** computers and other devices
- **personnel,** people who use, design, control or benefit from the system.

The components perform these basic functions:
- **input,** the data is collected and entered
- **processing,** data is changed or manipulated
- **output,** the results are shown
- **communication** and **feedback,** the results are sent out and new data is collected and entered in the system
- **memory** or storage of data.

B Types of systems

ICT systems are classified according to their aim.
- 'In our hospital we have set up an **information system** to manage data and information about our patients.'
- 'My house is an example of a **control system**. Its main aim is to control the different devices, e.g. switches that turn lights on and off as a security measure, sensors that detect smoke and set off the alarms, etc.'
- 'The Internet is a good example of a **communication system**; other examples are a mobile phone network or digital television. This type of system is designed for sending data between different devices.'

C Types of devices and services

At present most of the devices used in ICT systems are multi-purpose: mobile phones can be used as digital cameras or agendas, printers are also scanners and faxes. Not only is there media integration in the hardware, but also in the services offered by these telecommunication systems.

Call centres are one example of computer telephony integration where companies use databases and telephones for telemarketing.

Digital television uses digital technology to increase the number of channels and their quality of image. It also enables viewers to interact with the content and provide feedback to the programmer via telephone line, cable or satellite.

Teletext is a text-based information service provided by television companies. It uses part of the TV signal and is visible on sets with suitable decoders.

Faxes or **telefaxes** use telecommunication technology to send copies of documents through telephone lines.

Radio has also adopted the digital technology **DAB, Digital Audio Broadcasting**. Most digital radio stations are broadcast together with television signals.

The **Internet**, a global network of computers, enables users to exchange files, send emails and surf the Web to find information, take part in e-commerce, etc.

19.1 Fill in the diagram of components and functions of ICT systems with words from A opposite.

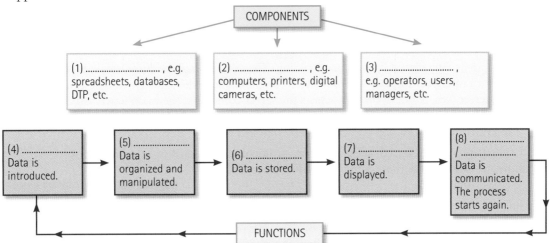

19.2 How would you define the following systems? Use the words in B opposite.

1 the registration system of a university
2 a robot at a car assembly line
3 an unmanned spaceship
4 a radio network
5 the *CIA World Factbook*
6 a video conferencing system

19.3 Solve the clues and complete the puzzle with words from C opposite.

Across
1 A new radio communication system.
3 A system that integrates telephones and computer is a .... centre.
4 A global system of networks of integrated services.
5 A device used to send and receive exact copies of documents.

Down
1 Similar to interactive TV.
2 Written information you get on your TV screen.

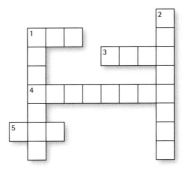

"Still nothing on the TV."

You and computers

Make a list of the ICT systems you use at work or at home. What is their purpose? What are their components?

20 Networks

LANs (Local Area Networks)

Networking allows two or more computer systems to exchange information and share resources and peripherals.

LANs are usually placed in the same building. They can be built with two main types of architecture: **peer-to-peer,** where the two computers have the same capabilities, or **client-server**, where one computer acts as the **server** containing the main hard disk and controlling the other **workstations** or **nodes,** all the devices linked in the network (e.g. printers, computers, etc.).

Computers in a LAN need to use the same **protocol**, or standard of communication. Ethernet is one of the most common protocols for LANs.

A **router,** a device that forwards data packets, is needed to link a LAN to another network, e.g. to the Net.

Most networks are linked with cables or wires but new **Wi-Fi, wireless fidelity,** technologies allow the creation of **WLANs**, where cables or wires are replaced by radio waves.

To build a WLAN you need **access points**, radio-based receiver-transmitters that are connected to the wired LAN, and **wireless adapters** installed in your computer to link it to the network.

Hotspots are WLANs available for public use in places like airports and hotels, but sometimes the service is also available outdoors (e.g. university campuses, squares, etc.).

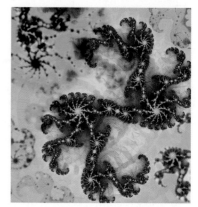

Networks

Network topology

Topology refers to the shape of a network. There are three basic physical topologies.

- **Star:** there is a central device to which all the workstations are directly connected. This central position can be occupied by a server, or a **hub**, a connection point of the elements of a network that redistributes the data.

- **Bus:** every workstation is connected to a main cable called a bus.

- **Ring:** the workstations are connected to one another in a closed loop configuration.

There are also mixed topologies like the **tree,** a group of stars connected to a central bus.

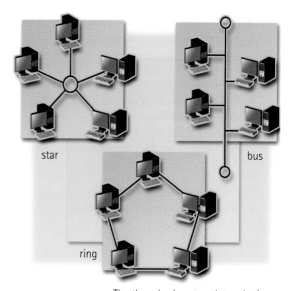

The three basic network topologies

WANs (Wide Area Networks)

WANs have no geographical limit and may connect computers or LANs on opposite sides of the world. They are usually linked through telephone lines, fibre-optic cables or satellites. The main transmission paths within a WAN are high-speed lines called **backbones.**

Wireless WANs use mobile telephone networks.

The largest WAN in existence is the Internet.

20.1 Read the information opposite and correct the following statements.

1 LANs link computers and other devices that are placed far apart.
2 In a client-server architecture, all the workstations have the same capabilities.
3 The word protocol refers to the shape of the network.
4 Routers are used to link two computers.
5 Access points don't need to be connected to a wired LAN.
6 Wireless adapters are optional when you are using a WLAN.
7 Hotspots can only be found inside a building.
8 The Internet is an example of a LAN.
9 Wireless WANs use fibre and cable as linking devices.

20.2 Use the words in the box to complete the sentences.

LAN	nodes	hub	backbones
WLAN	peer-to-peer	server	

1 All the PCs on a .... are connected to one .... , which is a powerful PC with a large hard disk that can be shared by everyone.
2 The style of .... networking permits each user to share resources such as printers.
3 The star is a topology for a computer network in which one computer occupies the central part and the remaining .... are linked solely to it.
4 At present Wi-Fi systems transmit data at much more than 100 times the rate of a dial-up modem, making it an ideal technology for linking computers to one another and to the Net in a ....
5 All of the fibre-optic .... of the United States, Canada and Latin America cross Panama.
6 A .... joins multiple computers (or other network devices) together to form a single network segment, where all computers can communicate directly with each other.

20.3 Read these descriptions of different physical topologies of communication networks and match them with the terms in B opposite.

1 All the devices are connected to a central station.
2 In this type of network there is a cable to which all the computers and peripherals are connected.
3 Two or more star networks connected together; the central computers are connected to a main bus.
4 All devices (computers, printers, etc.) are connected to one another forming a continuous loop.

20.4 A network administrator has set up a new network in a school. Which topology has she chosen?

We have decided to install computers in all the departments but we haven't spent a lot of money on them. Actually, only the one in the staff room is really powerful (and expensive!). They all have common access to the Net and share a laser printer. The teachers in this school have built up a general file of resources kept in the main computer to which all the others in the network have access.

"When I was a student, wireless data transmission meant passing notes in class."

 You and computers

Write a list of the advantages and disadvantages of using networks.

21 Faces of the Internet

A What the Internet is

The **Internet** is an **Inter**national computer **Net**work made up of thousands of networks linked together. All these computers communicate with one another; they share data, resources, transfer information, etc. To do it they need to use the same language or **protocol: TCP / IP** (**Transmission Control Protocol / Internet Protocol**) and every computer is given an address or **IP number**. This number is a way to identify the computer on the Internet.

B Getting connected

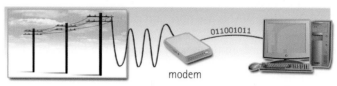

modem

Basic connection components

To use the Internet you basically need a computer, the right connection software and a modem to connect your computer to a telephone line and then access your **ISP** (**Internet Service Provider**).

The **modem** (**mo**dulator-**dem**odulator) converts the digital signals stored in the computer into analogue signals that can be transmitted over **telephone lines**. There are two basic types: **external** with a cable that is plugged into the computer via a USB port, and **internal,** an expansion card inside the computer. A **PC card** modem is a different, more versatile option for laptops and mobile phones.

At first most computers used a **dial-up** telephone connection that worked through the standard telephone line. Now a **broadband** connection, a high data transmission rate Internet connection, has become more popular: either **ADSL** (**Asymmetric Digital Subscriber Line**), which allows you to use the same telephone line for voice and fast access to the Internet, or **cable**, offered by most TV cable providers.

The basic equipment has changed drastically in the last few years. You no longer need a computer to use the Internet. **Web TV** provides email and access to the Web via a normal TV set plus a high-speed modem. More recently, 3Generation mobile phones and PDAs, personal digital assistants, also allow you to go online with **wireless** connections, without cables.

Telephone lines are not essential either. **Satellites** orbiting the earth enable your computer to send and receive Internet files. Finally, the **power-line Internet,** still under development, provides access via a power plug.

C Components of the Internet

The Internet consists of many systems that offer different facilities to users.

WWW, the **World Wide Web,** a collection of files or pages containing links to other documents on the Net. It's by far the most popular system. Most Internet services are now integrated on the Web.

Email, or electronic mail, for the exchange of messages and attached files.

Mailing lists (or **listservs**) based on programs that send messages on a certain topic to all the computers whose users have subscribed to the list.

Chat and **instant messaging**, for real-time conversations; you type your messages on the keyboard.

Internet telephone, a system that lets people make voice calls via the Internet.

Video conference, a system that allows the transmission of video and audio signals in real time so the participants can exchange data, talk and see one another on the screen.

File Transfer Protocol (FTP), used to transfer files between computers.

Newsgroups, where people send, read and respond to public bulletin board messages stored on a central computer.

TELNET, a program that enables a computer to function as a terminal working from a remote computer and so use online databases or library catalogues.

21.1 Read A and B opposite and decide if these sentences are *True* or *False*. If they are false, correct them.

1 The Internet and the World Wide Web are synonyms.
2 Computers need to use the same protocol (TCP / IP) to communicate with each other.
3 Web TV can provide access to the Net.
4 ADSL and cable are two types of dial-up connections.
5 External, internal and PC card are types of connections.
6 Information can be sent through telephone lines, satellites and power lines.
7 The computer IP number is a way to identify it on the Internet.

21.2 What Internet system from C opposite should these people use?

1 'I like receiving daily updates and headlines from newspapers on my computer.'
2 'I'm doing some research and need computer access to the University library.'
3 'I'd like to avoid flying to Japan to attend the meeting but I want to see what's going on there.'
4 'I want to read people's opinions about environmental issues and express my views.'
5 'I have designed a web page and want to transfer the data to my reserved web space.'
6 'I'd like to check my students' draft essays on my computer and send them back with my suggestions.'
7 'I don't want to spend too much money on international phone calls but I love hearing his voice.'
8 'I live in a small village where there are no other teenagers. I wish I had the chance to meet and chat with friends.'

21.3 Choose the correct alternatives to complete this newspaper article.

Sharing your broadband connection with your neighbours is either the best way of making friends or the fastest way to lose them. Thanks to new European legislation, (1) *modem / wireless / telephone* technology and a firm called MyZones, several households within 300 metres of each other can now share the cost of fast (2) *broadband / dial-up / phone* access. But the more people using your network, the slower it gets. If four people are using it at once, the surfing speed is 128k. Clive Mayhew-Begg, chief executive of MyZones, says: 'Sharing broadband is just the start of a new generation of consumer-based Internet services.' It starts on July 25 when MyZones will start selling £150 starter kits. These include a wi-fi (wireless technology) point and ADSL (3) *3G / modem / Web TV* but not the wi-fi adapters you and your neighbours will need. These will cost an extra £60 or so for each computer logged on to the wireless network. *The Mirror*

You and computers

How to choose the right ISP? How to decide whether you should change the one you have? Here are some decisions to make.

First of all you need to decide which type of connectivity (dial-up or broadband) you need depending on your requirements. Then the bandwidth (data transmission speed) they offer is another important factor. The services the ISP provides, such as the number of email addresses, space for web pages or blogs, spam and virus protection should also be taken into account. Last but not least, the cost of special software and connection fees should have an influence on your choice.

With these criteria in mind, have a look at some of the available ISPs and decide which one meets your needs best.

22 Email

What an email is

An **email** is an electronic message sent from one computer to another that can also include **attachments**: documents, pictures, sounds and even computer programs.

Although it's much faster and easier to use than the post, **snail mail,** the two have many things in common: you send an email to a **mail server** (an electronic post office) where it is stored in a **mailbox,** which holds incoming mail until the recipient downloads it. Users are given an **email address** and a password by an Internet Service Provider (ISP).

A typical **email address** has three parts.

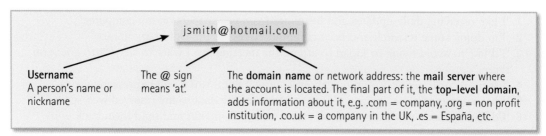

jsmith@hotmail.com

Username
A person's name or nickname

The @ sign means 'at'.

The **domain name** or network address: the **mail server** where the account is located. The final part of it, the **top-level domain**, adds information about it, e.g. .com = company, .org = non profit institution, .co.uk = a company in the UK, .es = España, etc.

Anatomy of an email

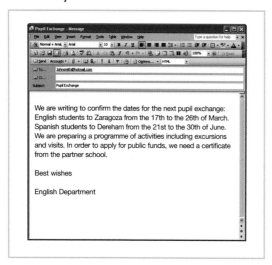

Emails usually have two main parts.

1. The **header** generally includes these:
   TO (name and address of the recipient)
   CC (carbon copy sent to another addressee)
   BCC (blank / blind carbon copy)
   SUBJECT (topic of the message)

2. The **body** (the message itself)

Some email programs also include a **signature,** with added information about the sender, at the end of the message.

You can make your message look more expressive or attractive by using **smileys** (also called **emoticons**): little pictures either made with characters from the keyboard such as :-) for happy, :-o surprised, :-(sad, etc. or downloaded images and animations.

Spam

Spam, or junk email, is the name given to unwanted messages, mainly commercial advertising. Some companies, **spammers,** use it extensively because it's cheaper than other types of advertising: you or your Internet Service Provider pay for it.

Mailing lists and newsgroups

A **mailing list** is a basic type of discussion group that uses email to communicate. The messages are distributed to all the subscribers, i.e. everyone who belongs to the list.

Newsgroups are similar. The main difference is that the message is not sent to someone's mail server but to a bulletin board where everybody can read and answer the message.

22.1 Find words in A and B opposite that match these definitions.

1 a file that has been included as part of an email message
2 conventional mail delivered very slowly in contrast with email
3 symbols used to express emotions in an email
4 the part of the email address that identifies the user of the service
5 the computer that provides you with mail service
6 a facility that allows users to send and receive messages via the Internet
7 the part of the email where you write the information about the addresses and subject
8 the part of the email address that identifies the server
9 the place where your Internet Service Provider stores new email for you

22.2 Look at the main parts of an email message in B. Where would you write the information below? What additional information do the TLDs (top-level domains) of the addresses give you?

1 peterswinburn@jazzfree.com
2 Eleanor Richardson
   Manager
3 maryjones@arrakis.es; susanwilt@hotmail.co.uk
4 Plane tickets
5 Peter,
   I've already booked the plane tickets to attend the Managers' Conference. Mary and Susan are joining us.
   Best wishes

22.3 A manager is giving his colleagues some advice on how to prevent spam. Complete the sentences with the words in the box.

mailing list	spam	email address	newsgroups	spammers

1 Never ever reply to a .... email or click on a link within the mail – this will lead to more junk email being sent to you. Unsubscribing only confirms you do actually exist, so they've hit the jackpot.
2 Don't let your email address be displayed anywhere on the Internet, including ...., chat rooms or any websites.
3 Never forward a spam to other people – .... might be able to track their addresses too, and you could end up losing friends!
4 Send your emails on a strictly 'need to know' basis; don't include everyone on a .... unless it is really necessary.
5 Treat your .... like your phone number – don't give it out randomly. Try to use a different one when shopping online.

> ## You and computers
> Smileys can make your email messages look much more expressive. Access the Web and download some for your future messages.

Married couple communicating via email at home

23 The World Wide Web

A What the Web is

The World Wide Web, Web or **WWW** is a network of documents that works in a **hypertext** environment, i.e. using text that contains links, **hyperlinks** to other documents.

The files, **web pages**, are stored in computers, which act as **servers.** Your computer, the **client,** uses a **web browser**, a special program to access and download them. The **web pages** are organized in **websites**, groups of pages located on the Web, maintained by a **webmaster**, the manager of a website.

The Web enables you to post and access all sorts of interactive multimedia information and has become a real **information highway**.

B How to surf the Web

To **surf** or navigate the Web, access and retrieve web pages or websites, you need a computer with an Internet connection and a web browser. After you have launched it, you must type the website address or **URL (Uniform Resource Locator)**, which may look like this:

> http://www.cup.org/education/sample.htm

http://   indicates the type of **protocol** that the server and browser will use to communicate. Here it is Hypertext Transfer Protocol.

www.   shows that it is a resource on the **World Wide Web**.

cup.org   is the **domain name** of the web server that hosts the website.

education   is the **path**, the place where a web page is located.

sample.htm   is the **filename** or name of a single web page.

The different parts are separated by full stops (.) and forward slashes (/). When we say a URL, we say **dot** (.) and **slash** (/).

To find interesting sites you can use **search engines**, where the website information is compiled by **spiders**, computer-robot programs that collect information from **sites** by using keywords, or through **web indexes**, subject directories that are selected by people and organized into hierarchical subject categories. Some **web portals** – websites that offer all types of services, e.g. email, forums, search engines, etc. – are also good starting points.

The most relevant website addresses can be stored in your computer using the **bookmarks** or **favourites** function in your **browser**.

Websites usually have a beginning page or **home** page. From this starting point you can navigate by clicking your mouse on hyperlinks in texts or images.

> BrE: favourites
> AmE: favorites

C What you can do on the Web

The Web is an open door to a universe of multimedia resources that people use in many different ways. Here are just a few.

> 'In my **weblog**, an electronic journal I maintain on the Web, you can read and post opinions in chronological order. In my role as **blogger**, the manager of a **blog**, I can promote this new type of discussion.'

> 'E-learning, education via the Web, is a great opportunity for people like me who haven't got time to attend classes.'

> 'Online shopping, i.e. **cybershopping** or **e-commerce**, saves you time and gives you the comfort of buying from your personal computer. The goods are then sent to you, so it's very easy.'

23.1 Solve the clues and complete the puzzle with words from the opposite page.

1 The WWW is also called the information ....
2 A link in a web page.
3 A website that offers a variety of services.
4 The first page of a website is the .... page.
5 A person who keeps a blog.
6 The manager of a web page is its web ....
7 An animal closely linked to the Web.
8 Another word for directory.
9 Another word for bookmark.

The hidden word is .... , text with links.

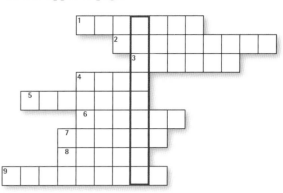

23.2 Complete these instructions about how to navigate with the words in the box.

client	web page	surf	web browser
search engine	web server	website	URL

1 Start up your computer and connect to the Internet.
2 Open your ....
3 Type the .... to access a website.
4 Your web browser sends the request to the correct ....
5 The server looks for the document and sends it to the .... computer.
6 Your web browser displays the selected .... on the screen.
7 From the home page of the .... you can .... to other pages by clicking on hyperlinks.
8 If you want to find more websites, use a ....

23.3 Some students accessed the websites below. What did they use the Web for? Use words from C.

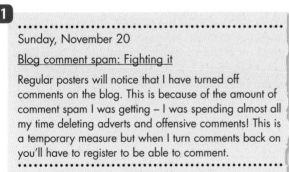

1

Sunday, November 20

Blog comment spam: Fighting it

Regular posters will notice that I have turned off comments on the blog. This is because of the amount of comment spam I was getting – I was spending almost all my time deleting adverts and offensive comments! This is a temporary measure but when I turn comments back on you'll have to register to be able to comment.

23.4 What are the main parts of this URL? How would you say the URL?

http://www.cambridgeesol.org/exams/cpe.htm

a .... b .... c .... d .... e ....

You and computers

URLs and email addresses are sometimes hard to say or can sound strange, e.g. www.dam.mit.edu. Access the *Professional English in Use ICT* website at www.cambridge.org/elt/ict. Then do the activity How to choose the perfect domain name.

24 Web design

HTML

Web pages are created with a special language **HTML (Hyper Text Markup Language)**, which is interpreted by a web browser to produce hypertext, a blend of text, graphics and links.

You can view the **source** or **raw HTML code** by choosing the *View Source* option in your web browser.

To build a website you could learn how to write **HTML tags**, the coded instructions that form web pages, or else use an **HTML editor**, a **WYSIWYG (What You See Is What You Get)** application that converts a visual layout into HTML code. A simpler option is to use a **web template** provided by a **web-based site builder**, where you just fill in the information you want on the page.

GOTHS

Goths like black and hate colour except red. You can tell them from other tribes by their white faces and sad, shy look.

You can find them in their black bedrooms writing poetry or posing dramatically on the dance floor, or perhaps buying more black clothes.

```
example.html
<!DOCTYPE html PUBLIC "-//W3C//DTD XHTML 1.0 Strict//EN"
   "http://www.w3.org/TR/xhtml1/DTD/xhtml1-strict.dtd">
<html xmlns="http://www.w3.org/1999/xhtml" xml:lang="en" lang="en">
<head>
   <meta http-equiv="Content-Type" content="text/html; charset=utf-8"/>
   <title>Goths</title>
   <style type="text/css" media="screen">
       body { font-family: "Comic Sans MS"; }
       img { float: left; margin: 0 120px; }
       h1 { font-size: xx-large; font-weight: normal; padding: 20px 0; color: red; }
       p { clear: left; font-size: medium; }
   </style>
</head>
<body>
<img src="goth.gif" alt="A Goth" width="72" height="90" />
<h1>GOTHS</h1>
<br />
<p>Goths like black and hate colour except red. You can tell them from other tribes by
their white faces and sad, shy look.</p>
<p>You can find them in their black bedrooms writing poetry or posing dramatically on
the dance floor, or perhaps buying more black clothes.</p>
</body>
</html>
```

Web page and raw HTML code

Basic elements

Some of the basic elements that can be found on a web page are:

- **Text**, which may be displayed in a variety of sizes, styles and fonts
- **Links**, connections from text or graphics on the current web page to different parts of the same page, to other web pages or websites, or to external files
- **Graphics**, pictures created with formats such as **JPEG (Joint Photographic Experts Group)**, which is ideal for pictures with a wide range of colours, e.g. photographs, and **GIF (Graphical Interchange Format)**, which is good for pictures with fewer colours or with large areas of the same colour, e.g. buttons, banners and icons
- **Tables**, intended for the display of tabular data, but often used to create page layouts
- **Frames**, subdivisions of a web page allowing the display of different HTML documents on the same page.

Instructions for the presentation, the styling of elements on a page such as text or **background** colour, can be included in the HTML code. However, it is becoming more common to use **CSS (Cascading Style Sheets)** to separate style from content. This makes pages easier to maintain, reduces download time and makes it easy to apply presentation changes across a website.

Video, animations and sound

Web pages can also include **multimedia files**: animations, audio and video files. Sounds are recorded with different audio formats. **MIDI, WAV, AU** and **MP3** are some of the most popular ones.

Shockwave and **Flash** are technologies that enable web pages to include video and animations.

Java applets, specific applications using that programming language, may be used to add interactivity to web pages.

To see or hear all these files, you need to download the right **plug-in**, the additional software that enables the web browser to support this new content.

24.1 Solve the clues and complete the puzzle with words from A opposite.

Across
4 What you see is what you get.
6 You can make a web page using an HTML
....
7 You just have to fill it in to create a web page.

Down
1 Templates are found in a web-based site
....
2 The instructions in HTML.
3 Another word for raw HTML code.
5 The language used to make web pages.

24.2 Complete this advice about web design with words from B opposite.

A well-designed website should be neat and organized. Words should be surrounded by sufficient white space. Use dark (1) .... on a light (2) .... , preferably white. You can divide the page into columns with a (3) .... or use (4) .... to create the page layout. Usually the navigation bar appears on the left side of the page. You can display it on all the pages of your website by using a (5) .... It is a good idea to put a (6) .... to the top of the page at the bottom of a long text.

The graphical element of a web page is crucial. (7) .... load slowly, so use them sparingly and for good reason. There are two common picture formats: (8) .... , for pictures with lots of colours and (9) .... , which is ideal for buttons and banners.

24.3 Look at C opposite. Match the sentence beginnings with the correct endings.

1 A plug-in is
2 Shockwave and Flash
3 Multimedia files can be included
4 Java applets
5 MIDI, WAV, MP3 and AU

a let you interact with information on the screen.
b usually needed to enjoy audio and video files.
c are some of the common audio formats.
d applications help to create animations.
e in web pages.

You and computers

Next time you surf the Web, look at the pages you visit in detail and decide if they are well designed.

■ What is it about the design that you find particularly useful or attractive?

■ Is there anything you don't like?

25 Chatting and video conferencing

A   IRC and web chat

IRC (Internet relay chat) is a system that allows Internet users to meet in **channels** (or **chat rooms**) in order to have live conversations on the topic of the chosen channel.

To participate you need to install a **chat client**, a special type of software, on your computer to connect to the **chat server**, the computer where the meeting takes place.

Once you have logged into an IRC server or a **web chat** site, you have to choose a username or **nickname** that will identify you during the chat.

After choosing the channel, you can read the conversations, type and send messages. You can post messages to everyone in the channel or have private conversations with someone.

Channels are run by **channel operators, 'chanops'** or just **'ops'** who control the content and the people who join and may ban users or ask them to leave the room.

B   Instant messaging

IM (instant messaging) programs allow Internet users to communicate in one-to-one conversations; they are a chat room for just two people.

With programs such as *ICQ (I seek you)* and *MSN Messenger* you can maintain a list of people, called a **buddy list** or **contact list**.

The program opens up a small window where the people engaged in the conversation type their messages.

The latest IM programs also incorporate telephone, video and file-sharing facilities and are becoming an alternative to traditional video conferencing programs.

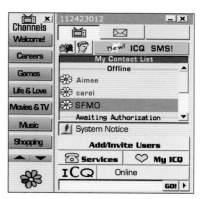

ICQ screenshot

C   Video and voice calls

Video conferencing (video call) systems allow a live connection between two or more participants in separate locations using the Internet to exchange **audio** and **video** data. The users need a computer with broadband access, a webcam, a microphone and speakers. Some popular programs are *CU-SeeMe* and *Windows Netmeeting*.

The Net can also be used for **online telephone conversations**, either computer-to-computer or computer-to-phone, which require special software (e.g. *Net2Phone*) or an **applet**, a Java application that runs from the browser when you access a web page, and also a microphone, sound card and speakers.

A video conference allows live visual and spoken communication

This type of communication uses **VoIP (Voice over Internet Protocol)**, which turns analogue audio signals, like the ones on the telephone, into digital data that can be sent via the Internet.

D   Virtual worlds

Internet users can also communicate in **three-dimensional** environments.

Instead of nicknames, people choose **Avatars** or **3D** characters in order to interact with other people.

A popular language used to create interactive simulations within the Net is **VRML (Virtual Reality Modelling Language)**.

Avatar image

25.1 Solve the clues and complete the puzzle with words from the opposite page.

1 One of the systems used for chat rooms.
2 The protocol needed for online phone conversations.
3 The language used to build virtual simulations.
4 Avatars are three .... characters.
5 Video calls transmit .... and video data.
6 Another word for channel operators.
7 You must install a chat .... on your computer.
8 The conversation takes place on a .... server.
9 A type of Java program whose name sounds like a fruit.
10 A synonym of a buddy list is a .... list.
11 Chats can also take place on the ....

1 _ _ C
2 _ o _ _
3 _ _ M _
4 _ _ m _ _ _ _ _ _ _ _
5 _ u _ _ _
6 _ _ _ n _ _ _
7 _ _ i _ _ _
8 c _ _ _
9 a _ _ _ _ _
10 _ _ _ t _ _ _
11 _ e _

25.2 Complete the sentences below with words from the box.

buddy	video conferencing	nicknames
chat room	messaging	avatars

1 Always show respect for other people in a .... Never send any unpleasant or threatening email messages.
2 Most instant .... programs have what is called a .... list. Each user's screen shows a box with the .... of the people he/she chats with.
3 The company hopes to have virtual open-plan offices, where researchers from around the world can collaborate. Individuals would be represented by .... , personalized electronic figures with perhaps a name badge or a picture of the owner's face.
4 Fear of flying is producing a surge of interest in .... , in which business people meet face-to-face even though they are hundreds or thousands of miles apart.

You and computers

There are certain netiquette rules you should follow if you want to use chat rooms and other communication environments correctly. Next time you enter a chat room, keep them in mind.

THE TEN NETIQUETTE COMMANDMENTS

1 Be polite. You're speaking to a human being not to a machine.
2 Don't use CAPITAL LETTERS! This is considered as shouting.
3 Have a look at the tone of the conversation in the room before you take part. You may not like that channel.
4 Ignore those people who don't follow these rules.
5 Don't believe all the things people might tell you. Some people lie just for fun.
6 Don't give personal information (your real name, address, password, etc.).
7 Protect your computer. Use a firewall and antivirus programs.
8 Don't accept files from people you don't know. They might be or contain trojans.
9 In short, follow the same rules as in real life.
10 Enjoy your chat and have fun!

26 Internet security

Internet crime

The Internet provides a wide variety of opportunities for communication and development, but unfortunately it also has its dark side.

Crackers, or black-hat hackers, are computer criminals who use technology to perform a variety of crimes: virus propagation, fraud, intellectual property theft, etc.

Internet-based crimes include **scam,** email fraud to obtain money or valuables, and **phishing,** bank fraud, to get banking information such as passwords of Internet bank accounts or credit card details. Both crimes use emails or websites that look like those of real organizations.

Crackers are a new type of criminal

Due to its anonymity, the Internet also provides the right environment for **cyberstalking,** online harassment or abuse, mainly in chat rooms or newsgroups.

Piracy, the illegal copying and distribution of copyrighted software, information, music and video files, is widespread.

But by far the most common type of crime involves malware.

Malware: viruses, worms, trojans and spyware

Malware (**mal**icious soft**ware**) is software created to damage or alter the computer data or its operations. These are the main types.

An email virus spreads through an email address book

- **Viruses** are programs that spread by attaching themselves to executable files or documents. When the infected program is run, the virus propagates to other files or programs on the computer. Some viruses are designed to work at a particular time or on a specific date, e.g. on Friday 13th. An email virus spreads by sending a copy of itself to everyone in an email address book.
- **Worms** are self-copying programs that have the capacity to move from one computer to another without human help, by exploiting security flaws in computer networks. Worms are self-contained and don't need to be attached to a document or program the way viruses do.
- **Trojan horses** are malicious programs disguised as innocent-looking files or embedded within legitimate software. Once they are activated, they may affect the computer in a variety of ways: some are just annoying, others are more ominous, creating a backdoor to the computer which can be used to collect stored data. They don't copy themselves or reproduce by infecting other files.
- **Spyware,** software designed to collect information from computers for commercial or criminal purposes, is another example of malicious software. It usually comes hidden in fake freeware or shareware applications downloadable from the Internet.

Preventative tips

- Don't open email attachments from unknown people; always take note of the file extension.
- Run and update **antivirus programs,** e.g. virus **scanners.**
- Install a **firewall,** a program designed to prevent spyware from gaining access to the internal network.
- Make backup copies of your files regularly.
- Don't accept files from high-risk sources.
- Use a **digital certificate,** an electronic way of proving your identity, when you are doing business on the Internet. Avoid giving credit card numbers.
- Don't believe everything you read on the Net. Have a suspicious attitude toward its contents.

26.1 Identify the Internet crimes sentences (1–6) refer to. Then match them with the advice below (a–f).

1 Crackers try to find a way to copy the latest game or computer program.
2 A study has revealed that half a million people will automatically open an email they believe to be from their bank and happily send off all their security details.
3 This software's danger is hidden behind an attractive appearance. That's why it is often wrapped in attractive packages promising photos of celebrities like Anna Kournikova or Jennifer Lopez.
4 There is a particular danger in Internet commerce and emails. Many people believe they have been offered a special gift only to find out later they have been deceived.
5 'Nimda' spreads by sending infected emails and is also able to infect websites, so when a user visits a compromised website, the browser can infect the computer.
6 Every day, millions of children spend time in Internet chat rooms talking to strangers. But what many of them don't realize is that some of the surfers chatting with them may be sexual predators.

a People shouldn't buy cracked software or download music illegally from the Internet.
b Be suspicious of wonderful offers. Don't buy if you aren't sure.
c It's dangerous to give personal information to people you contact in chat rooms.
d Don't open attachments from people you don't know even if the subject looks attractive.
e Scan your email and be careful about which websites you visit.
f Check with your bank before sending information.

26.2 Fill in the gaps in these security tips with words from the box.

digital certificate   malware   virus   scanner   spyware   firewall   antivirus

Malicious software, (1) ...., can be avoided by following some basic rules.

Internet users who like cybershopping should get a (2) .... , an electronic identity card.

To prevent crackers from breaking into your internal network and obtaining your data, install a (3) .... It will protect you from (4) ....

If you have been hit by a (5) ...., don't panic! Download a clean-up utility and always remember to use an (6) .... program, for example, a virus (7) ....

You and computers

1 What do you do to prevent computer infections?

2 Do you keep your virus protection updated? The Internet has lots of websites where you can get free advice and software. What should you do to improve your computer security?

Hey! Don't you think you're taking this virus scare too seriously?

27 E-commerce

A Elements of e-commerce

E-commerce or **online shopping** is the process of buying and selling products and services using the Internet. It has similarities with traditional commercial activity.

A product or service, from plane tickets to books, is offered in an **online shop,** the seller's website. Customers select and order products, which are then paid for and delivered. The main difference is that most of the processes take place on the Web.

Virtual shopping baskets keep a record of the items you buy

E-commerce websites use the following components:

- A **shopping cart program,** a web-based software application to keep a record of the products chosen by the customer.

- A **secure socket layer** (SSL) certificate, to verify that the credit card information has been securely transmitted; this is usually shown by a small padlock on the web page.

- A **payment gateway,** an interface between the website and the bank that accepts the electronic payment.

> BrE: shopping basket
> AmE: shopping cart

B How to buy on the Internet

The first thing to do is to look for the product in a search engine or, even better, in a **comparison engine** or bargain finder, to find the lowest price.

Most online shop websites are designed so that customers follow these steps to do their virtual shopping.

You start by adding the items you want to buy to the **shopping basket,** or virtual shopping trolley.

When you have selected the items that you want to buy, you proceed to the payment section by clicking on the **checkout button.**

You may have to **log in,** provide your username and password, or **sign up,** by providing your personal data, billing and shipping address, etc., if this is the first time you have accessed the site.

You will be given an **account,** so you are recognised as a customer. You will be asked to enter payment details, e.g. credit card numbers, etc. Before the transaction is completed you will be asked to confirm the order and check that all the information is correct.

Finally, you **log out** and leave the website.

Online shops offer a great variety of products and good prices

There are different types of electronic payment: credit cards or debit cards. A **digital wallet,** the electronic equivalent of a wallet for online shopping, holds credit card data and passwords for logging into websites. PayPal, Microsoft's Passport and Yahoo! Wallet are examples of digital wallets.

C Types of e-businesses

Companies whose activity is centred on the Internet are called **dotcoms,** after their web addresses. However, most e-commerce businesses are **bricks and clicks,** as they have both a physical and online presence.

Although there are some examples of **B2B** commerce, business to business, e-commerce is mainly used for **B2C,** business to consumer, or even for **C2C,** consumer to consumer. **Internet auctions,** websites like eBay where people offer products and sell them to the highest bidder, are an example of C2C e-commerce.

27.1 Solve the clues and complete the puzzle with words from A and C opposite.

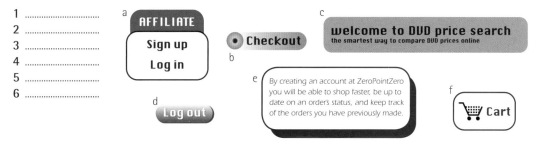

Across

1 One of the programs used to help shoppers while ordering on the Internet is called a .... cart program.
5 The most common type of e-commerce.
7 The exchange of goods and services over the Web.

Down

1 Type of certificate used to make credit card transactions secure.
2 An .... shop is an Internet shop.
3 The interface needed to pay online is a payment ....
4 The type of commerce that links two firms.
6 A type of e-commerce that some websites, e.g. eBay, have made popular.

27.2 Put these steps from shopping websites in the right order to explain the process of buying online.

1 ....
2 ....
3 ....
4 ....
5 ....
6 ....

a **AFFILIATE**
   Sign up
   Log in

b **● Checkout**

c **welcome to DVD price search**
   the smartest way to compare DVD prices online

d **Log out**

e By creating an account at ZeroPointZero you will be able to shop faster, be up to date on an order's status, and keep track of the orders you have previously made.

f **🛒 Cart**

27.3 There are some drawbacks to e-commerce and people are not always happy with it. Complete the sentences with words from the opposite page.

1 .... is great until you have a complaint. Unlike a shop you have nowhere to go.
2 There have been problems with both ...., web only businesses, and ...., high street names with a web presence. Computing experts say a large part of the problem lies with the software available for customer support online.
3 Since the National Consumers' League started tracking Internet fraud some years ago, one type of e-commerce has come top for complaints about fraud: Internet .... Four out of ten buyers reported problems such as never receiving what they had bid for.
4 If you want to reduce the risks while buying on the Web, use a .... as a way of holding securely credit card numbers, shipping and mailing addresses.

© Mike Baldwin / Cornered

"No thanks, just browsing."

> **You and computers**
>
> Have a look at different online shops. Study their design and the different elements they have used, and make a list of the type of products and services they offer.

28 Online banking

A | Online banking basics

Electronic banking is the general term given to the possibility of performing banking transactions through electronic communications, mainly the Internet. That's why many people prefer to use the terms **online banking** or **Internet banking**.

Online services can be provided by traditional banks, **brick-and-mortar banks**, which through the use of these new technologies become **brick-and-click banks**. Banks that don't have physical branches or ATMs are called **virtual** or **Internet banks**.

To use these services you need a computer with Internet access. Customers can also log in with a mobile phone or a PDA. The use of wireless networks to access financial institutions is known as **wireless banking**.

Brick-and-click banks are probably the best option to start with

B | Online banking services

What do you use online banking for?

'I **pay bills** online. I've got a list in my computer with all my payment recipients' names and account details. When I have to pay, I select the amount and the name of the payee. I can also **schedule the payments**, or fix the date for payments. The bank will **transfer the funds**, or send the money, to the selected account.'

'I **check account balances**. I can access and view my accounts any time, from any PC. Also, I don't need to wait for the post to get written statements from the bank. I can see and then **save online statements** on the bank's website. It saves time and paper.'

'I find online banking extremely convenient. I don't need to remember when my credit card expires or the date of a payment. My Internet bank **sends short message notifications**, warnings or other information services to my email or mobile phone.'

'I **trade stocks** online. I contact an online broker to invest my money, and to buy and sell shares.'

C | Online security

Most online banks have introduced the concept of **two-factor authentication**, the simultaneous use of at least two different devices or layers of security to prevent fraud.

When you open an Internet account, you are given a confidential **PIN, personal identification number**, and a password and username.

For some transactions, customers are required to use a **TAN, transaction authorization number**, from a list provided by the bank. It can only be used once, and it acts as a second password.

Security tokens are microchip-based devices that generate a number that has to be typed by the user or read like a credit card. They are becoming a common form of two-factor authentication.

One of the best methods of identifying the user of a bank account is **biometric authentication**, the use of a physical trait, such as a fingerprint, to allow a person to log in. Some laptops have built-in fingerprint readers, which makes online banking easier and more secure.

Security tokens provide a secure approach to online banking

28.1 Find expressions in A opposite which have the following meanings.

1 Banks that offer physical locations and online services.
2 The type of banking where you can use mobile phone networks to perform transactions.
3 Banks that only do business over the Internet. (*two possibilities*)
4 Banking services (transactions, payments, etc.) offered on the Internet. (*two possibilities*)
5 Banks that don't have a Web presence.
6 The general term that includes all sorts of banking that make use of ICT technologies.

28.2 Read B opposite and choose the right alternative for these electronic banking transactions.

1 *send / trade* stocks
2 *pay / save* bills
3 *check / trade* account balances
4 save *online statements / stocks*
5 transfer *short message notifications / funds*
6 schedule *funds / payments*
7 *pay / send* short message notifications

28.3 Complete this text with words from C opposite.

> Most financial institutions offering Internet-based products should use (1) ....-............................... authentication to reduce the risks of account fraud and identity theft.
>
> At present, most authentication methodologies involve three basic factors:
> • Something the user *knows* (e.g. a (2) ...., the confidential number given by the institution)
> • Something the user *has* (e.g. a (3) ...., the keyring–like identification number generator)
> • Something that shows who the user *is*, i.e. (4) .... authentication (e.g. a fingerprint).
>
> Authentication methods that depend on more than one factor are more reliable; for example, the use of a (5) ...., a TAN (something the user knows) to log in, and then a token (something the user has) to transfer funds.
>
> *Adapted from Federal Financial Institutions Examination Council*

"Jason feels insecure if he's too far from his money ... but electronic bank statements have cured that!"

29 | Mobile phones

cell

antenna and transceiver

Cells and base stations

A Mobile phones: definition and technology

Mobile phones, or **cellular phones,** are devices that enable communication to all types of telephones while moving over a wide area called the **coverage area.**

The term 'cellular' comes from the fact that the phone calls are made through **base stations,** communication towers or antennas, which divide the coverage area into **cells.** As you move from cell to cell, the calls are transferred to different base stations belonging to the same or a different telephone company. This capability of mobile phones is called **roaming.** The phone is said to be **out of range** when it cannot communicate with a base station.

B A brief history

> BrE: mobile phone
> AmE: cellular phone

- **1G, First Generation** phones started in the 1980s when Motorola introduced the first hand-held phones. They used analogue technology and the main drawback was the small number of channels that could be used at a time.
- In the 1990s, **2G** mobiles introduced **digital** transmission methods that converted voice into binary information, increasing the number of channels, the speed of transmission between the phone and the base station and enabling a reduction in size. The most common standard, **GSM, Global System for Mobile communications,** started to be used at this stage. One of the features of this technology is the use of **SIM cards,** a type of smart card that contains the user's information, the connection data and the phonebook. It also enables the user to change service provider without changing the handset.
- **3G** phones offer a high-speed data transfer capability. Some of these phones are called **smart phones** and combine PDA capabilities with the usual functions of a digital phone. The new communication standard, **UMTS, Universal Mobile Telecommunications System,** enables the multimedia transmissions that are becoming common nowadays.
- New standards are being developed that will open the way to new **4G** phones with an emphasis on multimedia, real-time television and radio.

C Features and functions

Mobiles have become an essential part of our lives and there are many uses for them.

> 'I've bought a new mobile with **Bluetooth,** a wireless technology, to connect my phone to other devices at home or in my office. It also has **WAP, Wireless Application Protocol,** which enables access to the wireless Web, and an integrated **PDA,** a digital assistant, where I keep my appointments and sales records.'

> 'My mobile has **programmable ring tones,** so I can personalize my phone's melodies or sounds, and **changeable faceplates,** which make the front look different. I used to just send **SMS (short message service),** short text messages. Now I can also take and send pictures with the **built-in digital camera.'**

> 'I'm mad about music, so I love having a mobile which integrates radio and **MP3,** the most usual music file format on the Web. I can download music from the Net and listen to it on my mobile.'

> 'I'm very concerned about safety in the car. That's why I bought a **hands-free kit,** so I can drive and talk on the phone without taking risks.'

> 'This mobile also has a **speakerphone:** I can talk without holding the handset. I also use it when I want several people to participate in the call.'

29.1 Complete this text about basic principles of mobile telephony with words from A opposite.

> Mobile phones, also called (1) .... , or cell phones for short, need a network of towers or antennas to transmit calls. In a cellular system, a city is divided into smaller sections or (2) .... where the (3) .... usually occupy a central position. When you are outside your service provider's (4) .... area, your telephone may become out of (5) .... unless your telephone allows (6) .... , i.e. the ability to use another service provider's network.

29.2 Read B opposite and decide if these sentences are *True* or *False*. If they are false, correct them.

1 1G phones had a slower transmission speed than 2G.
2 2G phones introduced analogue technology.
3 GSM started to be used in the 80s.
4 Smart phones can be used for other purposes, e.g. as a personal digital assistant.
5 People won't be able to watch live TV on 4G phones.
6 SIM cards enable users to keep important information.
7 UMTS, the standard used in 3G phones, has made video phones a commercial reality.

29.3 Read C opposite and match the CNET.com phone reviews (1–5) to the descriptions of users who might be interested in them (a–e).

1 This is the best multimedia phone, with a 1.3-megapixel digital camera, TransFlash card slot, Bluetooth and an MP3 player.

2 This is the best smart phone, with wireless support (Bluetooth and Wi-Fi), WAP and email.

3 This model is the best phone for SMS addicts, with a QWERTY keyboard and multiple messaging options.

4 This is the best status-symbol phone, with a striking design, beautiful display and speakerphone; it's a world phone. Hands-free kit included.

5 This phone is the best for teens, with an eye-catching pop-up display, vibration feedback for game playing, programmable ring tones and changeable faceplates.

a People who love talking, playing games and unusual ring tones

b People who prefer writing to phoning

c Phone users who love taking pictures and watching videos, and music lovers

d People who want email and to surf the Web

e Mobile phone fanatics who travel a lot and want to make an impression

---

You and computers

Mobiles can be very annoying for people around you if you don't follow certain rules. In addition, they may be harmful for your health. Access the *Professional English in Use ICT* website at www.cambridge.org/elt/ict. Then do the activity <u>Are you a responsible mobile user?</u>

30 Robots, androids, AI

A Robots and automata

A **robot** is a computer-programmed machine that performs actions, manipulates objects, etc. in a precise and, in many cases, repetitive way.

Robots may be **automata**, or man-like machines, whose basic components are similar to a human body.

- They have mechanical links, **joints**, which connect their movable parts.
- Their heart and muscles are the electric or pneumatic motors or systems, the **actuators**, which create the movement.
- Robots also have hands, usually tools or grippers, called **end effectors**.
- They may be equipped with cameras or infrared controls, **sensors**, which transmit information to the central system in order to locate objects or adjust movements.
- Finally, robots depend on a **computer system**, the brain that directs the actions.

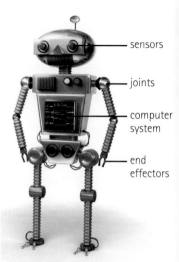

sensors

joints

computer system

end effectors

B Uses for robots

The word *robot* comes from *robota*, meaning compulsory labour in Czech; similarly, robots are helpful in activities which are too dangerous, too boring or too precise for human beings.

Robots in industry

Robotic arms, telescopic or bending arms, are widely used in the automobile industry to paint, weld and assemble car parts. Robots are also used in electronic assembly of microchips where precision of movements is essential.

Robots and space

Planetary rovers, remotely-operated vehicles, and **space probes**, unpiloted spaceships, are used to explore space.

Robots and health

Surgical robots, which help human surgeons, are programmed to assist in very delicate microsurgery operations or mimic the surgeons' movements in telesurgery operations.

Robots and safety

Mobile robots, vehicles controlled by human operators, are used for defusing bombs and handling hazardous materials.

Robotic arms are common in industry

C Artificial Intelligence

Artificial Intelligence (**AI**) is the science that tries to recreate the human thought process and build machines that perform tasks that normally require human intelligence. It has several applications.

Androids are anthropomorphic robots designed to look and behave like a human being. Most androids can walk, talk and understand human speech. Some react to gestures and voice inflection. Some 'learn' from the environment: they store information and adapt their behaviour according to a previous experience.

Expert systems is the term given to computer software that mimics human reasoning, by using a set of rules to analyze data and reach conclusions. Some expert systems help doctors diagnose illnesses based on symptoms.

Neural networks are a new concept in computer programming, designed to replicate the human ability to handle ambiguity by learning from trial and error. They use silicon neurons to imitate the functions of brain cells and usually involve a great number of processors working at the same time.

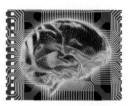

Artificial Intelligence?

An android and a human being: can you tell one from the other?

30.1 Complete the article with words from A opposite.

> ## ACTION ROBOT TO COPY HUMAN BRAIN
> Scientists at Aberystwyth University are working on a machine which they hope will recognize objects with cameras that will work as (1) .... , and retrieve objects with an arm that will be its (2) ....
> Although the arm will have (3) .... that will link its muscles and an electric motor that will be the (4) .... , this new (5) .... won't move like a human, i.e. it won't be like the (6) .... of science-fiction films: forget *Star Wars'* C3PO. It will be desk based: no walking, or climbing stairs.
> The team hopes to discover how the brain performs 'multi-tasking' and to use that information to develop the (7) .... to create a robot that can think for itself.

30.2 Match the pictures below to the types of robots in B opposite.

30.3 Complete the extracts with words from C opposite.

The term (1) .... is defined as the automation of intelligent behaviour, but can (2) .... really be intelligent?

(3) .... are made of units that resemble neurons. They are often used to simulate brain activity and are effective at predicting events.

(4) .... , also known as knowledge-based systems, mirror the structure of an expert's thought.

You and computers

Make a list of other uses of robots at home and at work.

31 | Intelligent homes

Domotics

Domotics, from the Latin word *domus* plus **robotics**, also known as **automation**, involves the use of information technology applied to domestic appliances in order to create intelligent systems inside the house.

Basic **intelligent devices**, traditional devices with an embedded processor, have been with us for a while, e.g. microwave ovens and washing machines with computerized controls.

Intelligent homes are a wider concept: all the systems and devices are connected in a LAN, local area network, where they communicate with each other and are controlled by a central computer sometimes installed in one of the machines.

B | Control devices and networking

Intelligent homes are controlled with different types of **interfaces**, devices that facilitate communication between the user and the system: physical switches, touch screens, IR (infrared) remote controls, computers either at home or at a distance, telephony.

The different elements perform one of these two functions: they are either **command initiators**, e.g. a brightness sensor that is programmed to send an instruction when it gets dark, or **command receivers**, e.g. a light that turns on when it receives an instruction sent by the sensor.

Household appliances, sound and video systems, optical and thermal sensors, etc. can be linked with **wired** and **wireless** systems. Wired LANs use different types of cables and also electrical wiring.

WLANs, wireless networks, use radio-frequency systems: **Bluetooth**, a short-range radio system used to communicate between portable devices (laptops, PDAs, mobile phones, etc.), is now frequently used to design **PANs** (**personal area networks**) inside the home.

C | Automatic operations

Intelligent systems are able to perform a series of activities to improve these areas.

Security	● Turn on and off alarm systems and phone emergency services if needed
	● Open and close doors and gates, blinds or curtains
Safety	● Control heat and smoke sensors
Comfort and economy	● Control heating, air conditioning and electricity
	● Detect motion and switch on and off lights accordingly
	● Switch on and off hi-fi sets and home cinema; select music and programs
	● Have everything ready when you wake up: the bath running, the electric kettle on, the news headlines on your computer, etc.
	● Keep a list of the products in the fridge, make an order to a supermarket and suggest recipes
	● Provide intelligent garden watering, e.g. only when the soil is dry
Assistive technology	● Raise and lower motorized cupboards and sinks for people with mobility problems

31.1 Solve the clues and complete the puzzle with words from A and B opposite.

Across

3 A wireless standard used for PANs.

6 Touch screens, remote control and computers are different types of ....

7 The adjective which describes networks without cables.

9 A smoke sensor is an example of a command ....

Down

1 The automatic operation of a system or process.

2 The term domotics comes from *domus* and ....

4 The adjective used to describe homes and devices that use IT technology.

5 A light switch can be used as a command ....

7 LANs where the devices are connected with cables or electrical wiring are ....

8 Personal Area Network.

31.2 Read the text and answer the questions below.

'Smart' homes not far away

Picture this scenario: it is a Friday night in the middle of winter and you are driving to your holiday home in the mountains for the weekend. On your way there, you send your second residence a text message which will activate the heating, so the place is nice and warm by the time you arrive. Your main residence, meanwhile, may be vacant, but you can send it an SMS to turn the lights on and off a few times, giving the impression to potential burglars that someone is there. You can also monitor what is happening inside the house on your mobile phone – cameras inside the house will send real-time images direct to your phone. If disaster strikes, and the washing machine leaks while you are not there, your house is so clever that it will automatically turn off the water at the mains and alert you that a plumber may need calling.

Sounds far-fetched? For one family of four, these are the capabilities their home already has. They are living in an Eneo Labs show home outside Barcelona, trying out the company's smart home concept. Javier Zamora, manager of Eneo Labs, says that in as little as two years many of us will be enjoying these features. He explains that smart homes have two main components: an 'information network', which is like a human body's nervous system in that all devices inside the house are connected to it; and a 'brain', which coordinates what is inside the home and connects it to what goes on outside. He says that in the future the house will respond to voice commands.

Adapted from www.cnn.com

1 Which of the areas in C opposite are improved in this 'smart' home: security, safety, comfort and economy, assistive technology? Which one is not?

2 What operations is the system able to perform to improve those areas?

3 What interface is used to connect the user to the LAN? What might be used in the future?

> **You and computers**
>
> Would you like to make your home intelligent? Access the *Professional English in Use ICT* website at www.cambridge.org/elt/ict. Then do the activity Your dream home.

Build your dream home

32 Future trends

A Smaller and faster

Nanotechnology, the science of creating and using materials or devices at molecular and atomic sizes, is going to represent a new technological revolution. These devices will fall in the range of 1 nanometre, which is equal to one billionth of a metre, to 100 nanometres (nm).

Nanobots, robots formed from molecules or molecular components, will be used in medicine to control and diagnose diseases. For example, they will be injected and will move through blood vessels destroying cholesterol molecules or cancer.

Nanocomputers, molecule-sized computers, may have the power of 100 workstations but only be the size of a grain of sand. There will be two main types of molecular computers:

Artist's impression of a nanobot on a red blood cell

- **Quantum computers**, based on quantum mechanics, may be millions of times faster than current computers. They will be so fast because they will be able to examine all possible answers to a query at the same time. This capability is made possible by qbits, **quantum bits**, which can be 0 or 1, or something in between, simultaneously.
- **DNA computers** will use **DNA biochips** to perform the same functions as silicon microchips do today but at a much faster speed.

B Computers everywhere: human-centred technologies

The relationship between people and computers will be closer.

Computers will be **embedded**, or hidden, in a variety of items. For example, we'll have **wearable computers** that will be embedded in a belt or a piece of jewellery, etc.

User interfaces, the systems that facilitate communication between people and computers, will resemble human communication. There will be **gesture interfaces** based on facial-hand recognition systems.

ICT devices will be mobile and multimedia: we'll watch **mobile TV** programmes on our phones, which will also access the Internet and work as a mobile office.

Computer chips can be injected under the skin: **RFID, radio-frequency identification tags**, might be used to track or identify people or to store information, such as medical data, although there are concerns about privacy and personal safety.

In the near future we'll be able to swim in the **immersive Internet**, a technology that will change the two-dimensional world of the Internet into a 3-D experience with three-dimensional sound and images and even the sense of touch.

By the year 2040 there might be **intelligent robots**, machines that will be able to think creatively. The processing power of computers may have reached 1,000,000,000 **MIPS (millions of instructions per second)**, the estimated speed of human thought.

32.1 Read these extracts and replace the words in *italics* with words in A opposite.

1 A *computer of this type* is a molecular computer that works biochemically. It 'computes' using enzymes that cause chain reactions.

2 In a *computer of this type*, data is processed by exploiting the strange qualities of quantum physics; the building blocks of computation are not transistors but caged atoms or qbits.

3 *It* has the potential to revolutionize the way we live, from creating miniaturized 'Star Trek'-like electronic gadgets to delivering medicines to specific places within the human body.

4 The government plans to fund a study examining the feasibility of *molecule-sized robotic devices* that would position atoms to build complex substances and products.

5 Scientists at an Israeli institute have developed a *very small one* – so small that a trillion of its kind fit into a test tube.

32.2 Write a caption under each picture illustrating the future trends from B opposite.

1 .... 2 .... 3 ....

4 .... 5 .... 6 ....

32.3 Match the terms with their definitions.

1 quantum bits   a a microchip made with organic materials
2 DNA biochip   b the speed at which the CPU processes instructions
3 embedded   c the device or program used to interact with a computer
4 user interface   d subatomic particles used in quantum computers
5 MIPS   e fixed, integrated

You and computers

Access the *Professional English in Use ICT* website at www.cambridge.org/elt/ict.
Then do the activity Emerging technologies.

33 Prefixes

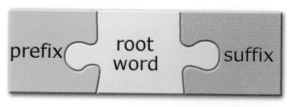

Word parts are like puzzle pieces

A Common prefixes

We can form new words by using prefixes and suffixes, e.g. <u>micro</u>-process-<u>or</u>

prefix + root + suffix.

Prefixes come before the root word and usually change its meaning. Here are some common ones in ICT.

- Negative prefixes meaning 'not':
  - **non-** **Non-volatile** memory retains its content when the power is turned off.
  - **un-** An **unformatted** disk has not been 'initialized'; it doesn't allow data to be stored.
- Prefixes of location:
  - **trans-** (= across) Data **transmission** can be wired or wireless.
  - **inter-** (= between) The Internet consists of millions of computers **interconnected** in a global network.
  - **intra-** (= within) An **intranet** is a private network, restricted to a company's internal use.
  - **extra-** (= outside, in addition to) An **extranet** links a company with its customers and suppliers.
  - **tele-** (= over a distance) **Teleconferencing** enables users in different places to talk to and see each other.
- Prefixes of size:
  - **super-** (= large, better) A **supersite** offers links to other websites on a certain topic.
  - **semi-** (= half, partly) A **semiconductor** is neither a good conductor nor a good insulator (e.g. silicon, used to make computer chips).
  - **micro-** (= small) A **microbrowser** is designed to display web pages on PDAs and mobiles. Prefixes of size are also used in units of memory like *megabyte* and *gigabyte*.
- Another common prefix is **re-** in words like *reprint*, *rewritable* and **reboot**, to start the computer again.

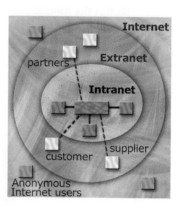

An extranet is like an extended intranet

B Verb prefixes

Prefixes used to form verbs which mean 'to cause to be something':

- **en-** **encrypt**: to change data into a secret code so that only someone with a key can read it
- **up-** **update**: to modify data in a file and thus ensure the file reflects the latest situation
  upgrade: to add or replace hardware or software in order to expand the computer's power
  upload: to send files to a central, often remote computer; compare with 'download'

Prefixes that mean 'the opposite of an action' or 'to reverse an action':

- **de-** **decrypt**: to convert secretly coded (encrypted) data back into its original form
  decompress: to restore compressed data back to its original size
  debug: to correct errors in a program or system
  defragment: to reorganize data stored on disk by putting files into contiguous order
- **un-** **uninstall**: to remove hardware or software from a computer system

C The prefixes e- and cyber-

The e- prefix means 'electronic'; **cyber-** describes things relating to computer networks.

- **e-** The term **e-learning** refers to the use of ICT to provide education and training.
  An **e-zine** is a magazine or newsletter published online.
  E-commerce is the buying and selling of products or services over the Internet.
- **cyber-** The electronic space in which online communication takes place is called **cyberspace**.
  Cyberslacking means using a company's Internet access for activities which are not work-related, e.g. emailing friends, playing games, etc.; it is also called 'cyberloafing'.

33.1 Use words from A opposite to complete these sentences.

1 Medical researchers in many countries exchange information through email and ....
2 .... memory (e.g. ROM or flash memory) is able to hold data when switched off.
3 Blogs and web portals are examples of .... ; they offer news, opinions and web links.
4 .... are used for making integrated circuits and computers.
5 I'll post the agenda for next week's meeting on the company's ....
6 A home network is two or more computers .... to form a local area network.

33.2 Complete these definitions with words from A opposite.

1 .... : a disk that is completely blank, so information can't be recorded onto it
2 .... : a network that allows communication between a company and the people it deals with
3 .... : the process of sending data over a communication channel
4 .... : to restart the computer, without switching it off completely
5 .... : a web browser designed for small screens on hand-held devices

33.3 Complete these sentences with words from B opposite and make any necessary changes.

1 The program ran so slowly, I had to un............................... it.
2 Your financial information is fully en............................... and cannot be accessed.
3 Messages encrypted using a public key can only be de............................... by someone with the corresponding private key.
4 The computer compresses and de............................... a colour image in less than a second.
5 Once you've written a program, you have to test it and de............................... it to remove all the errors.
6 In cyberspace, 'up...............................' means to send a file.
7 You can easily up............................... your files by adding or deleting information.
8 To de............................... your hard disk you need a disk optimizer, a program that will reorder your files.
9 There are minimum system requirements for your PC to be suitable for .... to Windows Vista.

33.4 Complete this text with words from C opposite.

The term 'cyber' first appeared in the word 'cybernetics', coined by Norbert Wiener in 1948 as the science of communication and control. In the 1960s new 'cyber' words emerged, such as *cybermen* and *cyborg*, referring to a being that is part robot, part human. In 1984 William Gibson popularized the term (1) .... in his novel *Neuromancer*. He used it to describe a futuristic, virtual world of computers, but now it refers to the Internet. Other common words are *cyberworld*, *cybercafé*, and *cyberphobia* (a fear of computers). Companies are now worried about (2) .... : employees using the Net to do things that have nothing to do with their jobs, e.g. chat with friends.

A cybercafé

The e- prefix is often added to activities that have moved from the physical world to the electronic alternative, e.g. *email* and *e-shopping*. Other well-known examples are: (3) .... , small magazines that are available on the Internet; (4) .... , doing business electronically on the Net; and (5) .... , providing instruction via optical discs, the Web or satellite TV.

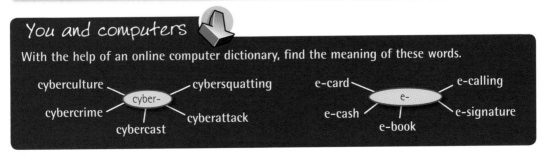

You and computers

With the help of an online computer dictionary, find the meaning of these words.

cyberculture — cyber- — cybersquatting
cybercrime — cyberattack
cybercast

e-card — e- — e-calling
e-cash — e-signature
e-book

34 Suffixes

Common suffixes

Suffixes change the class of the root word. For example, by adding the suffix **-er**, the verb *publish* becomes the noun *publisher*. Suffixes can tell you if a word is a noun, adjective, verb or adverb.

Suffixes for jobs:

-er	*manufacturer* *webmaster*	The two major **manufacturers** of processor chips are Intel and AMD.
-eer	*engineer* *auctioneer*	Greg is a **software engineer**, which means he writes computer programs.
-or	*animator* *operator*	He worked as a computer **animator** on *Toy Story*.
-ant	*IT consultant* *IT assistant*	She's a **computer consultant** and specializes in e-commerce, data protection and IT strategies.
-ian	*technician* *electrician*	A **computer technician** installs, troubleshoots and upgrades hardware and software.
-ist	*typist* *scientist*	Anyone who works as a **typist** may develop a problem with their hands.

Other common suffixes in ICT:

Nouns	**-ion, -ment, -ics, -ity** (activity, state)	compression, management, robotics, electricity
Adjectives	**-able, -ible** (able to be)	programmable (keyboard), convertible (format)
	-ful (full of), **-less** (without)	colourful, colourless (picture)
Verbs	**-ize, -ise** (to make)	synthesize (music – to make it with a synthesizer)

B Word families

It is useful to know how to build up word families by adding suffixes. Look at these examples:

Nouns	Verbs	Adjectives	Adverbs
magnet, magnet**ism**	magnet**ize**	magnet**ic**, magnet**ized**	magnet**ically**
record**er**, record**ing**	record	record**able**, record**ed**	
digit**izer**, digit**izing**	digit**ize**	digit**al**, digit**ized**	digit**ally**

Adding a suffix may change the pronunciation. Look at how the stress changes in these words:

p<u>ho</u>tograph   phot<u>o</u>grapher   photogr<u>a</u>phic   photogr<u>a</u>phically

C We love 'wares'

The suffix **-ware** refers to products of the same type. In computing, *software* refers to programs executed by a computer, as opposed to the physical devices on which they run – the *hardware*. It is commonly used to form jargon terms for classes of software.

Be careful of spyware!

- **freeware**: available free of charge, but protected by copyright; it differs from 'free software', which can be changed and distributed subject to licence
- **shareware**: distributed similarly to freeware, except that it requires payment after a trial period
- **malware**: designed to infiltrate or damage a computer (e.g. viruses, trojan horses, spyware)
- **spyware**: designed to monitor the actions of your computer and send this data via the Net
- **adware**: devised to display advertisements; some includes spyware
- **groupware**: enables a group of people connected to a network to work on the same project

34.1 Which IT professionals from A opposite are described here?

1 a person who designs and maintains software applications
2 a person who gives expert, professional advice
3 a person who uses graphics software to make or edit animated pictures
4 a person who is employed to type letters, reports and other documents
5 a person or enterprise that produces goods in large numbers, using machines
6 a specialist in the technical details of computers

34.2 Complete each sentence using the word in brackets and the correct suffix from A opposite.

1 IBM's BlueGene is the most .... supercomputer. (POWER)
2 Most library databases are .... via the Internet. (ACCESS)
3 I'll email my report to you as an .... (ATTACH)
4 This book will show you how to .... your small business. (COMPUTER)
5 An .... optical disc allows data to be deleted and new data to be recorded on it. (ERASE)
6 The growth of the Internet has increased the need for effective data .... (SECURE)
7 The combination of .... and new textile materials has made it possible to create musical jackets and smart shirts that can read our heart rate. (ELECTRON)
8 Bluetooth is a .... technology designed to connect computers, mobile phones and other devices, replacing direct cable links. (WIRE)
9 Aircraft flight .... is used to train pilots. (SIMULATE)

34.3 Look at the word families in B opposite and complete these sentences with the correct word.

1 From kitchen magnets to computer disks, ... plays a central role in the technology of everyday life.
2 Hard disks are .... storage devices.

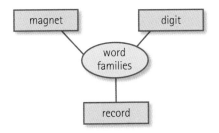

3 My digital voice .... has a storage capacity of 2 GB.
4 Blu-Ray Disc is a new .... optical disc format developed by nine electronic manufacturers.

5 A video .... is used to convert analogue video into digital video files.
6 Sound and pictures can be stored .... , as on a CD.

34.4 Look at C opposite. What type of software do these descriptions refer to?

1 software that transmits data about your Web surfing habits without your consent
2 also known as 'try before you buy' software
3 short for malicious software
4 software that periodically pops up advertising material
5 collaborative software
6 programs that you don't have to pay for

"Do you still refuse to run pirated software?"

35 Compounds

A Compound nouns

Compound nouns consist of two or more words used together as a single word, e.g. *hard drive*.

In a compound there is a headword and one or more modifiers.

| *ink-jet* | *printer* |
| modifier | head |

Modifiers can refer to different things:

- material, e.g. **silicon chip** = a chip made of silicon
- use or function, e.g. **search engine** = a program used to find information on the Web
- activity or profession, e.g. **software engineer** = a person who designs software
- place, e.g. **web portal** = a site on the Web that acts as a gateway to other sites

Compound nouns are written in different ways:

- as two separate words, e.g. **control panel** = a utility that lets you configure and adjust a system
- as two words joined with a hyphen, e.g. **self-test** = an automatic examination of a device
- as one word, e.g. **clipboard** = a holding place for text or graphics you've just cut or copied

Unfortunately there are no rules. For example, you may see *clip art*, *clip-art* and *clipart*. Some compounds change over time, for example two words – *web site* – become hyphenated after a time, and then eventually end up as one word – *website*.

The two parts may be:

1 noun + noun	**address bus** = a set of wires that identifies locations, addresses, in the main memory
	bandwidth = the rate at which data flows through a cable or network
	mail merge = a tool that combines a standard letter with a mailing list to create personalized letters
2 adjective + noun	**broadband** = high-speed connection, e.g. cable or ADSL Internet access
	shortcut = a small file, 1KB in size, that links to a real file stored elsewhere
	smart card = a plastic card that contains a small chip
3 verb or verbal noun + noun	**scrollbar** = part of a window that lets you move through a document
	recording head = a mechanism that transfers data to a disk
4 verb + particle	**add-on** = a hardware or software module that can be added to a computer
	set-up / setup = the way in which a program or device is configured

Compound nouns normally have the main stress on the first part and a secondary stress on the second part, e.g. screen saver /ˈskriːn ˌseɪvə(r)/.

B Compound adjectives

Compound adjectives are made up of two words, normally with hyphens between them. The second part is often a past participle.

A **menu-driven** program lets you select a command from a menu.
A **voice-activated** product is activated by the user's voice.
Object-oriented programming is based on objects and their effects on each other, rather than on a series of instructions.

Other common patterns include:

- noun + present participle
Space-saving PCs take up very little desktop space.

- noun + adjective
A **hands-free** device does not require the hands for operation.
A **stand-alone** computer or business can operate on its own.

An experimental robot receiving voice-activated instructions

35.1 Look at A opposite. Which compound do these definitions refer to?

1 a small piece of silicon which is used in computers
2 a site that offers email, news, forums, web searching, online shopping and links to other sites
3 a utility used to adjust computer settings such as fonts, sound and networks
4 the read/write head of a disk drive
5 a computer bus used by the CPU to communicate memory locations

35.2 Complete these sentences with a compound from A opposite.

1 .... enables you to combine two files, one containing names and addresses and the other containing a non-specific letter intended for multiple recipients.
2 A USB headset is a useful .... , the ideal accessory for your computer games and music.
3 The printer's .... didn't identify any errors.
4 Because the Web has no central organization, every Web surfer needs a ....
   – a special site that locates other sites based on words or phrases you type in.
5 They are seeking a .... to help write and test a new operating system.

35.3 Complete the puzzle with compound nouns.

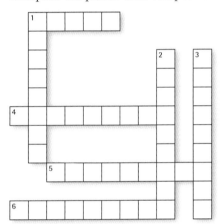

Across
1 the configuration of hardware and software
4 a bar that allows you to select the portion of the document you want to see
5 an area that holds the things you copy, ready to be pasted anywhere else
6 a type of data transmission that provides fast Internet access

Down
1 a special file which redirects to another file or program
2 a small card with an embedded microchip
3 the amount of data that can be transmitted along a channel

35.4 Complete these sentences with a compound adjective from B opposite.

1 A .... - .... telephone allows people with limited mobility to dial and answer the phone with just the sound of their voice.
2 A fax machine is a .... - .... device, so it does not require any other device to function.
3 A .... - .... application is operated by making choices from menus instead of giving instructions on a keyboard.
4 In some countries it is obligatory to use a .... - .... car kit when you are using a mobile phone while driving.
5 An .... - .... language like C++ lets the programmer concentrate on individual units (e.g. a piece of text, a graphic or a table) and give each object functions which can be changed easily.
6 They've launched a new .... - .... computer, an entire PC embedded inside a keyboard.

A space-saving PC

You and computers

Access the *Professional English in Use ICT* website at www.cambridge.org/elt/ict.
Then do the activity <u>Combinations with 'card' and 'web'</u>.

36 Collocations

A What a collocation is

A collocation is a pair or group of words that are often used together. You need to learn them in order to sound natural in English. For example, in computing we say **'attach a file'**, not 'enclose a file'.

New collocations are particularly common in ICT. Notice the combinations that are worth learning from these reviews.

With the Nokia 770 Internet Tablet you can **browse your favourite sites** and catch up on your email – from right where you are. Whether you're relaxing on the sofa or enjoying the moment at your favourite café, if you have **broadband access** over Wi-Fi, the Nokia 770 Internet Tablet gives you instant wireless access to the Web. You can also **stream**[1] **files, tune in to Internet radio** and News Reader, or **play** your favourite **videos** and **music**.

[1] *Listen to audio or watch video directly from the Internet rather than downloading and saving it first*
[2] *Able to share data with older systems*

A Blu-ray Disc is a new **optical disc** that provides five times more data storage than a DVD, with a capacity of 25 GB (single-layer), 50 GB (dual-layer) and 100 GB (four-layer). Unlike current DVDs, which use a red laser to **read and write data**, Blu-ray uses a blue laser (which is where the format gets its name). Blu-ray discs can record and play back **high-definition television** and digital audio, as well as computer data.

Blu-ray Disc players are **fully backward compatible**[2] with CD/DVD formats. They also let users **go online** and download subtitles.

B Some types of collocations

Verb + noun
> The easiest way to **connect to the Internet** is by using a DSL modem.
> A DSL modem can **transmit data** at high speed.
> Your ISP will probably give you a CD with instructions on how to **install the software** on your PC.
> Once you are online, you can **access the Web** or **send and receive emails**.
> You may like to **burn CDs**, i.e. copy your favourite songs or important files onto CDs.

Verbs with particles
> Can you show me where the microphone **plugs into the computer?**
> If you want to **log onto your account** you will need your user ID and password.
> Computer criminals are getting better at **hacking into** other people's **computers**.

Adjective + noun
> **High-speed networks** and multimedia phones allow customers to view live TV.
> To send **outgoing mail** and retrieve **incoming mail**, you need to configure the email settings.
> Most teenagers use **instant messaging** to chat with friends.
> **Electronic commerce** – from a PC, digital TV or mobile phone – offers competitive prices.
> **Wireless hotspots** provide Wi-Fi Internet access in airports, hotels and other places.
> Users can interact with a **virtual environment** through the use of VR displays and data gloves.
> Typical **interactive TV** uses are voting in polls, video on demand and shopping from home.

Adverb + adjective
> Don't send **highly sensitive information** via email or fax unless it is encrypted.
> This movie is **freely available** on the Internet, so it can be downloaded free of charge.

Phrases
> When you chat in a chat room, you are interacting in **real time** since it is immediate.
> A USB device is a good example of **plug and play**; you install it and use it immediately.
> To **drag and drop**, just click on the object and drag it to a different location.

36.1 Look at A opposite. Match each word on the left with its partner on the right.

1 high-definition   **a** Internet radio
2 read and write   **b** disc
3 play   **c** videos and music
4 tune in to   **d** television
5 broadband   **e** data
6 optical   **f** your favourite sites
7 browse   **g** compatible
8 fully backward   **h** access

36.2 Answer these questions using collocations from B opposite.

1 What sort of locations or access points can be used to surf the Net without wires?
2 What feature allows an electronic device to be used as soon as it is connected to a computer?
3 If you are *gaining illegal or unauthorized access to computer data*, what are you doing?
4 If you want to move a picture to a new location, what do you do?
5 What expression is used to refer to personal, confidential or classified information?

36.3 Read these statements by computer users and complete them with suitable collocations.

1 'I have a program that monitors both incoming and .... mail and also blocks spam.'
2 'With a webcam you can add video to online chats and .... messaging. Simply .... the software included, plug the webcam .... your PC, and start having video conferences.'
3 'This software enables you to burn .... and DVDs containing any data files.'
4 'I use a media player to .... audio and video files from the Web; I can play them directly.'
5 '*NetMeeting* allows us to perform video conferencing in .... time, without any delay.'
6 'We have decided to make the material .... available on the Web.'
7 'I often log .... my Internet bank account to make payments; I never forget to log off.'

36.4 Complete the collocations in this text.

Fast connections
Connecting to the (1) .... using DSL lines, cable TV and satellite increases bandwidth dramatically, making the Web more useful. Increased speed has ignited an explosion of (2) .... commerce, video on demand, telecommuting, collaborative scientific projects, video conferencing and (3) .... environments.

Internet2, shaping the future
Internet2 is not a single network, but a consortium of hundreds of (4) .... networks linked by fibre-optic backbones that span the United States and link to other countries. The network transmits (5) .... at speeds up to 2.4 gigabits per second – 45,000 times faster than a 56 Kbps modem – allowing scientists to test their laboratory discoveries in the real world.
     The next-generation network went (6) .... in February 1999, linking a number of universities around the world. When it is in commercial use, services will be available like (7) .... television, virtual 3-D videoconferencing, and much more.

A new kind of Web
While PCs were once the primary means of accessing the Internet, we're now seeing Internet-enabled devices such as PDAs and cell phones that send and receive (8) .... and access the (9) .... Soon, everything from your car to your refrigerator will be connected to the global network, all communicating with each other wirelessly.   *www.learnthenet.com*

You and computers

Access the *Professional English in Use ICT* website at www.cambridge.org/elt/ict.
Then do the activity <u>Word combinations relating to mobile phones</u>.

37 Defining and classifying

A Describing function

We define an object by describing its function and properties.
For example, we can define a 'router' like this:

> A router is a <u>device</u> **used to** transmit data between two computers or networks.

Internet   modem

A wired router

There are other ways of describing its function:
- **for +** *-ing* (**for transmitting**)
- relative pronoun + verb (**which/that** transmits)
- relative pronoun + **is used + to +** infinitive (**which/that is used to** transmit)

We can define people and places like this:

> A blogger is a <u>person</u> **who** keeps a Web log (blog) or publishes an online diary.
> An address bar is the <u>area</u> in your browser display **where** the web address is displayed.

- We use **which** or **that** to refer to things.
- We use **who** or **that** to refer to people.
- We use **where** (= at which) to refer to places.

A wireless router
is a <u>device</u> **which**
allows computers to
communicate via radio
waves

B Classifying from general to specific

'Classifying' means putting things into groups or classes. We can classify types of music, parts of a computer, classes of software, etc.

Typical expressions

> ... **are classified into** X **categories**
> ... **can be divided into** X **types**

> ... **include**
> ... **consists of**
> ... **is made up of**
> ... **is composed of**
> ... **comprise**

> types
> There are X classes of ...
> categories

Examples: classifying storage media

Storage media **are** often **classified into three categories**: magnetic, optical and flash memory.

Magnetic storage media **include** tape cartridges, floppies and hard disks.

A hard disk **consists of** several disks (platters) and their read-write heads.

Optical storage media **comprise** CDs, DVDs and high-definition video discs, which **include** two competing formats: HD-DVD and Blu-ray.

There are two basic types of flash memory: flash memory cards – used in digital cameras – and USB flash drives, also called pen drives.

C Classifying from specific to general

We can also classify from the specific to the more general. We can say, for example, that 'a word processor (*specific*) is a type of software (*general*)'.

Typical expressions

> ... **is a type of**
> ... **are parts/components of**
> ... **constitute**
> ... **make up**

Examples

OCR **is a type of** software which recognizes characters.

A PC card radio and a router **are** two basic **components of** a wireless network.

The RAM and the ROM **constitute** the main memory.

The **System** and **Finder** programs **make up** the Mac OS.

37.1 Look at A opposite. Match the two halves to make correct definitions.

1 A web browser is a program   a where emails are kept when they are received.
2 A host is a computer   b used for displaying web pages.
3 The inbox is the location   c who is new to an activity such as using a PC or the Internet.
4 A ripper is a piece of software   d used to provide data and services to other computers.
5 A newbie is somebody   e which is used to extract files from a CD/DVD and convert them to other formats.

37.2 Correct the underlined errors in these definitions. Use *who*, *that*, *which* or *where*.

1 Mobile TV Broadcasting is a system <u>who</u> lets you watch TV on a PDA or mobile phone.
2 A computer geek is someone <u>which</u> is an enthusiastic user of computers, sometimes to an obsessive degree.
3 The Recycle Bin is the folder <u>that</u> deleted files are stored until you decide to delete them completely.
4 Digital Terrestrial TV is a technology <u>where</u> allows you to receive more channels and a better picture through a conventional aerial instead of a satellite dish.

37.3 Look at B and C opposite. Underline all the classifying expressions in this text.

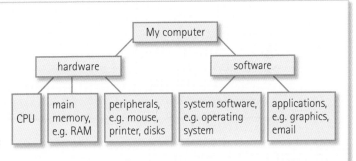

Computer organization

A computer consists of hardware and software. The CPU, main memory and peripherals constitute what is known as hardware – the physical parts. The control unit, the arithmetic-logic unit and the registers are the basic parts of the CPU. The RAM and the ROM make up the main memory. Peripherals are classified into three types: input, output and storage devices.

Software can be divided into two categories: (i) system software, which includes operating systems, programming software and system utilities, and (ii) application software, which comprises programs that let you do specific tasks (e.g. graphics, email).

37.4 Complete the sentences with a classifying expression from the box.

there are two types of ...	... is composed of	... is a type of
... are made up of	there are four main classes of ...	

1 .... microchips: (i) microprocessors, used as CPUs in computers, (ii) memory chips, used to store data, (iii) digital signal processors, used in mobiles and digital TVs, and (iv) application-specific integrated circuits, used in cars and appliances.
2 In the future, people may have biochips inserted under their skin. Biochips .... two components: a small chip, called a transponder, and a scanner.
3 A network .... two or more computers connected together to share information and resources.
4 .... network architecture: peer-to-peer, where all PCs have the same capabilities, and client-server (e.g. the Internet), where servers store and distribute data, and clients access this data.
5 Bluetooth .... wireless technology for transferring data between devices.

You and computers

Draw a diagram classifying the hardware and software components of your PC. You can use exercise 37.3 to help you. Include as many details and devices as possible.

38 Qualifying and comparing

A Choosing a computer

How to make the right decision

What to look for in a computer? How much do I need to spend? Where should I start?

Top Personal Computer hopes to help you make the right decision.

The first question you have to ask yourself is what you'll use the computer for. Then you can decide what system will fit your needs by considering the following factors:

You need expert advice when buying a new computer

- The quality you need and the price you are willing to pay: you can buy a **low-end**, mid-range or **high-end** computer.
- Three basic features make a big difference: the CPU speed, the amount of RAM and the size of the hard drive. To run **highly demanding** applications you'll need a **fast** processor, **plentiful** RAM and a **spacious** disk.
- If you already have peripherals and software, you'll have to ensure they are **compatible** and can be used with the new computer.
- If you want to use the system for some time, it should be **expandable**, i.e. it should allow you to add on new peripherals.
- Most standard computers offer **integrated**, built-in, sound cards. If you're keen on music you should also buy **separate**, external, speakers.
- Finally, make sure the system you buy is **reliable**, i.e. it's not likely to go wrong. Check that you will receive a warranty and good technical support.

B Comparing qualities

Comparing and finding differences or similarities are common functions in ICT. When you want to buy a new device, or you read articles about the latest computer or mobile phone, or need to make a decision about the most suitable ICT system for you, you may have to use and understand expressions like the ones in these examples.

Comparison

A flat-panel monitor is	**slimmer**	**than**	a CRT.
A PDA is	**more** manageable	**than**	a laptop.
Laser printers offer	**higher** quality	**than**	ink-jet models but
ink-jet printers cost	**less** money.		
You can type	**more** easily		with a separate keyboard.
Free programs are	**as** good	**as**	proprietary ones.
A broadband line is	**the best** option		to download multimedia.

The more memory you have, **the** faster you'll be able to load your files.

Contrast

While a dial-up connection is usually cheap, it is very slow.
A scanner can be useful **but** it isn't an essential peripheral.
Unlike CRT monitors, TFT ones are light.

Similarity

Both brand name **and** clone computers have **similar** features.
Online shops **as well as** local retailers offer good value hardware.

While consoles are a better option if you just want to play games, PCs support more applications and are easier to upgrade

38.1 Complete the extracts with adjectives from A opposite.

> I wanted a powerful computer to work with (1) .... multimedia applications, so I decided to buy a (2) .... computer with a (3) .... microprocessor, good graphics and sound cards and (4) .... RAM.

> I didn't know whether to buy a new or a used desktop. I just need it to write documents, but I was advised to buy as much as I could afford. Finally I bought a (5) .... but new desktop with 256 megabytes of memory, enough for my needs.

> I didn't want my new computer to become outdated too quickly. That's why I made sure it would be easily (6) .... with enough space for add-in cards.

38.2 Complete these sentences with adjectives from A opposite.

1 Although many computers on the market have hard disk drives with a capacity of 80 to 160 GB, many home users want more .... drives because of their need for additional storage.
2 This 'Wireless Enterprise Communicator' is the first realistic alternative to carrying around .... devices. It offers an .... mobile phone, GPS, barcode reader and hand-held computer.
3 Before you subscribe to a music subscription service, make sure you have a .... player that supports the music formats available.
4 Systems and devices are becoming more and more .... because reliability means manufacturers save money by having fewer tech support calls.

38.3 Complete the text about the advantages and disadvantages of laptops and desktops with words from B opposite.

> (1) .... desktops and laptops have (2) .... components but they are built in a different way.
>
> (3) .... desktops have (4) .... space to expand the system, they are less manageable (5) .... laptops. On the other hand, laptops are fully portable: they are lighter and (6) .... and so more practical if you travel a lot and need to take your computer with you.
>
> (7) .... desktops, the screen, keyboard and mouse of a laptop are integrated. However, most laptop owners prefer to have a separate mouse (8) .... the touchpad. Similarly, as the keyboard is miniaturized, some people buy an external one for use at home. You can type (9) .... easily if you use a full-size keyboard.
>
> A laptop's CPU is slower (10) .... access to data may be quicker, so its performance can be (11) .... good as a desktop's.
>
> It's hard to say what the (12) .... option is. But remember: in the computer world, (13) .... smaller the device, the more money it costs.

You and computers

Access the *Professional English in Use ICT* website at www.cambridge.org/elt/ict. Then do the activity <u>Compare before you buy</u>.

39 Describing technical processes

A A technical process: how VoIP works

With VoIP, Voice over Internet Protocol, your voice **is digitized** and then broken into small data packets.

To make a phone call, an analogue telephone must **be hooked up**, linked, to an ATA, an analogue telephone adaptor. When you pick up the receiver and dial a number, the tones **are converted** by the ATA to digital data and temporarily stored. When your friend picks up the phone, a session **is set up,** established, between both computers. During the conversation the systems transmit packets of data that are sent back and forth through your VoIP company's call processor. They are received by the ATA and converted to the analogue audio signal that you hear. When you hang up, a signal is sent by the ATA to finish the session.

VoIP calls can also be delivered via an IP telephone with an Internet connection. *Adapted from* How Stuff Works

ATAs enable online telephony

When describing a technical process, we often use the present simple passive, e.g. *is digitized / are converted / is set up*, to explain how something is made or used. The agent is not as important as the process. Compare these sentences:

Active	Passive
Someone *sets* up a session.	A session *is set* up.
The ATA *receives* packets.	Packets *are received* by the ATA.

B The use of the passive

The passive is often used to describe areas of computing. Look at these examples:

Input, process, output

The data **is fed into** the computer system. Instructions **are processed** by the CPU. The results **are displayed** on the monitor.

Storage

Today a lot of information **is held**, kept, on optical discs.

The data in the hard disk should **be defragmented**, rearranged, so it can be accessed more quickly.

Computer components and configuration

The icons and taskbar can **be customized**, configured, to cater for your needs.

Your computer system may need to **be upgraded**, improved, by adding devices or updating software.

Internet

Messages **are posted,** sent, to a newsgroup where they **are threaded**, grouped, by subject.

Files can **be uploaded**, transmitted, to another computer by using FTP, File Transfer Protocol.

C Sequencing a process

The use of time and sequence connectors means we can show the different stages of a process.

Typical connectors	Examples
First ... Then / Next ... Finally ...	**First** the computer is switched on. **Then** the OS is booted. **Finally** the application is run.
As ...	**As** the laser printer drum rolls, the toner gets stuck to it and reproduces the original image.
After / Once ...	**After** you have had a program for a while, it may have to be updated. **Once** a CD-R has been written to, you can't alter the data.
Before ...	**Before** you can recover the files that have been deleted, you must unformat the hard disk.

39.1 Complete the sentences with verbs from A and B opposite.

1 In order for your voice to travel over the Net as email does, it must be .... from an analogue to a digital signal, i.e. it must be .... , and then broken into small envelopes of data called Internet Protocol packets. Voice communication that is .... in this way is what's known as Voice over IP.

2 The Pocket Weather Tracker, which is the size of a mobile phone, measures temperature, humidity and barometric pressure. The results are .... on an easy-to-read LCD screen.

3 One football coach who uses high-tech training methods says: 'We have 11 cameras strategically positioned on the stands and they film an entire match. Then the recording is .... into a main computer and 24 hours later we have a CD-ROM disc which presents everything in a tactics board format.'

39.2 Solve the clues and complete the puzzle with verbs from A and B opposite.

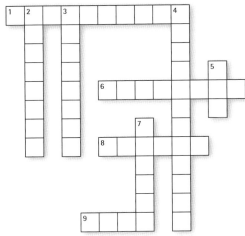

Across

1 It has been .... , i.e. laid out according to the user's specifications or needs.
6 The web page will be .... to the server, where it will be published.
8 Different peripherals can be .... up to a PC.
9 More data is .... on a DVD than on a CD.

Down

2 After my computer had been .... by adding more RAM, it had better performance.
3 In an Internet discussion group the messages are .... in reply to an initial post.
4 The disk was .... to optimize the data storage.
5 A video conference was .... up to present the new products to the customers.
7 A lot of responses to that controversial message were .... to the newsgroup.

39.3 Rearrange the paragraphs in the text below by referring to the connectors in C opposite.

a Then a pure silicon crystal is cut into thin wafers, which are covered with two other layers of protective materials.

b First engineers design the construction plans for the chip.

c After the chemical treatment, the chip undergoes a process that alters its electrical properties.

d Chip production today is based on photolithography. Here is a sequential description of the process.

e Finally when all the components are ready, metal is added to connect the components to each other.

f Next UV-light is shone through the mask and onto the wafers. The protective materials break apart on the parts of the chip that are hit by light. Then it has to be treated with chemicals before the protective material can be removed.

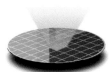

UV-light is shone through the mask and onto the wafers

You and computers

With the help of the information in this unit, explain the process you follow when you want to write a document using your computer. You might need the following verbs:

switch on   boot up   run   type in   edit   insert   save   print   switch off

40 Troubleshooting

A Troubleshooting and help desks

Sally Harrison is a **help desk technician**. She works at a **help desk**, a computer support centre where people phone for help with their computer problems.

'In my job I have to talk to the computer user to find the source of a problem and try to fix it on the phone.

We offer computer assistance for all types of problems. Some people prefer to use the word **debugging** when we solve programming errors and use **troubleshooting** when we solve problems encountered while using information technology tools.

Sometimes there are no problems with either of them and it's a PEBCAK, the problem exists between the chair and keyboard, i.e. it's a user's problem.

I generally start by asking the customer if there has been an **error message**, a warning of a problem displayed by the application inside a **dialogue box**, a small window that provides information about the problem and an interface of communication with the user.

One of the most frightening messages is the one shown with a BSoD, or Blue Screen of Death, a blue screen that shows an unrecoverable system error.'

B Describing the problem

People ask the help desk technician for help with problems like these.

1 'My printer is producing **fuzzy**, not clear, printouts.'
2 'I get a lot of error messages. Some of my files won't open. They're **corrupted**, damaged.'
3 'The monitor **flickers**, the image is unsteady.'
4 'My optical drive **fails**: it won't read or write discs.'
5 'My machine is running very slowly and it shows **low memory** error messages.'
6 'My computer is behaving strangely. I think it's got a **virus**.'
7 'I get a 401 message: I'm **unauthorized**, not allowed to enter that website.'
8 'I've tried to access a website but I get a 404 **Not Found** message, as if it didn't exist.'
9 'I try to connect but I get this message: **Network connection refused by server**.'

C Making guesses and giving advice

Help desk technicians have to sort out the different reasons for the problem and suggest ways to fix it. Look at some of the expressions that can be used.

- **Turn** the computer **off** and on again. It often works.
- You should check that dust is not affecting the computer **cooling fan**, the device that prevents the parts inside the computer from overheating.
- Why don't you **reboot**, restart, the system again?
- If this doesn't work, use a **recovery tool**, a software application to restore your deleted data.
- You should **back up** your files in the future, make copies.
- If I were you, I'd get a **UPS**, an **uninterruptible power supply**, a device to maintain the continuous supply of electric power.

40.1 Complete these sentences with words from A opposite.

1 Your computer may have a virus if it has symptoms like these:
Windows won't start and an .... tells you that it's because important files are missing.
An unfamiliar message pops up in a .... The message is usually unrelated to programs you're running or asks for confidential information such as passwords.

2 A bug is a coding error in a computer program. That's why some people say that .... is the art of taking bugs out – programming is the art of putting them in.

3 The company is improving the .... for computer users. They are introducing 'answer-express' to handle all kinds of technology support and online advice.

4 The firm is seeking a .... to join the team. The successful candidate will be responsible for .... and resolving problems for internal staff as well as external users.

40.2 Match the pieces of advice (a–i) with the problems (1–9) in B opposite.

a Haven't you got any antivirus software installed? If I were you, I'd try a free online scan.
b Why don't you reset the refresh rate of your monitor?
c You may have made a mistake while typing your password. You can't access a website if you aren't recognized as a guest. Try typing it again.
d The computer may be overheating. Check there's nothing blocking the flow of air. You should also use a recovery tool to retrieve your files.
e Your system must be running short of memory. You'd better add some more RAM.
f That message shows the web server is busy. Why don't you wait and try again later?
g Your discs or perhaps your lens might be dirty. Use some special disc polish.
h It might mean that the page is no longer on the Internet. Check the URL again. If that doesn't work, you could use a search engine to find similar pages.
i The print heads of your printer must be clogged, obstructed with ink. Run the clean cartridge routine or wipe them with a cloth and distilled water.

40.3 Here are some preventative tips to stop disasters before they start. Complete the text with words from C opposite.

■ Your PC has a mortal enemy: heat. Since the most common cause of overheating is dirt, you should ensure that your CPU (1) .... doesn't become clogged by cleaning it with compressed air.

■ Check your power protection: if there are frequent voltage spikes or power outages in your area, get a (2) .... to power your PC.

■ Remember your (3) .... software is essential so you won't lose important information. It's always essential to (4) .... all the files you'll need in the future.

■ Evaluate your hard disk's health with its error-checking utility.

■ Finally, if disasters do happen, remember that it's always useful to (5) .... off and on the computer or (6) .... the OS.

Adapted from PC World Magazine: 'Complete PC Preventive Maintenance Guide'

You and computers

Have you (or any people you know) had any of the problems described in this unit?
Make a list.

Answer key

0.1 Nouns: Internet, design, microchips (print can also be a noun)
Verbs: print, design
Adjectives: financial, electronic

0.2
1 design	3 microchips	5 financial
2 Internet	4 print	6 electronic

0.3
1 microchips	3 financial	5 Internet
2 design	4 electronic	6 print

0.4
1 teleworking	4 translation of *switch on*	6 communicator
2 calculating	in your language	7 mobile phone
3 calculations	5 interact, (teleworking)	8 typewriter

0.5 1 a   2 d   3 e   4 c   5 b

You and computers

Possible answers

> 1 **hardware (COMPUTER)** /ˈhɑːd.weəʳ/ US /ˈhɑːrd.wer/ *noun* [U] the physical and electronic parts of a computer, rather than the instructions it follows
>
> 2 **software** /ˈsɒft.weəʳ/ US /ˈsɑːft.wer/ *noun* [U] the instructions which control what a computer does; computer programs: *He's written a piece of software which calculates your tax returns for you.*

(Cambridge Advanced Learner's Dictionary)

1.1
1 screen reader	3 interactive whiteboard
2 head-mounted display	4 GPS, DVD recorder

1.2
1 virtual reality	2 assistive technology	3 wireless network

1.3
1 technological dependence	3 electronic waste	5 cybercrime
2 computer addiction	4 loss of privacy	

1.4
publishing:	design online newspapers, publish e-books
home:	surf the Web, download files, retouch photos
banks:	make calculations, store information
offices:	write letters and faxes, send emails

You and computers

Possible answers
At work, I use computers:
- to write letters and memos
- to make calculations and graphics
- to keep records of clients and suppliers
- to find out information on the Web
- to communicate with other companies or institutions via email or video conferencing
- to prepare business presentations
- to store information and do tasks related to my job

In my free time, I use computers:
- to play games
- to retouch photographs
- to download music from the Web
- to chat with friends and relatives
- to watch video clips and full-length movies
- to do online shopping

2.1   1 CPU (central processing unit)   3 monitor   5 webcam
       2 mouse   4 printer   6 keyboard

2.2   1 c   2 b   3 d   4 a

2.3

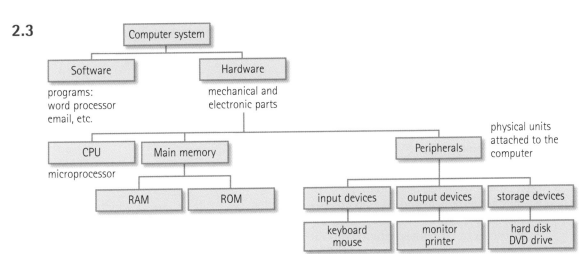

2.4

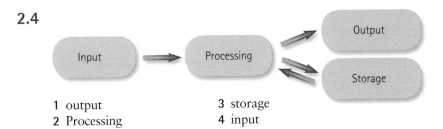

    1 output   3 storage
    2 Processing   4 input

3.1   1 personal digital assistant / PDA   4 wearable computer
       2 desktop PC   5 laptop / notebook
       3 mainframe   6 tablet PC

3.2   1 a laptop / notebook   4 USB (Universal Serial Bus) ports
       2 a TFT screen   5 a Lithium-ion battery pack
       3 a touchpad

3.3   1 hand-held   4 voice recognition
       2 stylus   5 handwriting recognition
       3 touch screen   6 wireless

You and computers

Possible answers

1 Benefits of PDAs:
  - they can be carried and used easily
  - with wireless technologies, they can access email or the Internet anytime, anywhere
  - they can exchange (synchronize) data with desktop computers
  - they are cheaper than notebooks / laptops
  - pen-based systems can recognize handwritten characters

  Limitations of PDAs:
  - they are not powerful enough to run high-demanding applications
  - they have limited storage capacity
  - they may use batteries very quickly
  - they have small screens, so it's not possible to display large tables or charts
  - they may cause hand problems because of the small buttons

2 Benefits of laptops for business people:
  - they are ideal for executives and for people who travel a lot
  - they can be just as powerful as desktop PCs, with the additional benefit of freedom to move about
  - they allow business people to transfer data, share services and communicate with the central office easily
  - they are very useful for business presentations

3 Using tablet PCs in the classroom:
  - they are ultra-light and take up little space, so they can easily be integrated into classes
  - they enable learners and the teacher to 'write and draw' using digital ink
  - learners can take notes with a stylus rather than a keyboard
  - they can access the Internet via Wi-Fi (wireless) connection
  - they can record audio files, such as a class lecture, to review later
  - teachers can install interactive e-learning programs about different subjects
  - they can convert their notes to slides for electronic projection

4.1
1 joystick	4 mouse	7 lightpen
2 scanner	5 graphics tablet	8 digital camera
3 barcode reader	6 microphone	

4.2
1 trackball	3 webcam
2 touch screens	4 touchpad

4.3
1 alphanumeric keys	6 Caps Lock
2 function keys	7 Backspace
3 dedicated keys	8 Ctrl
4 cursor keys	9 Enter / Return
5 numeric keypad	

4.4
1 double-click	3 right-click
2 click	4 drag

You and computers

Possible answers

1 The system converts voice into text, so you can dictate text into programs. The technology is particularly useful for dictating notes, memos, letters, emails, etc.
You can also control the computer with voice commands; this means you can start programs, open files, save them in a particular format or print them, etc.

Some systems let you surf the Web or chat using your voice instead of the keyboard.
The system helps blind people and other disabled users to communicate with their computer.

2 In the future, a lot of people will use their voices to interact with computers. The idea of talking to a computer naturally (like a friend) seems reasonable. It will probably be very popular and a lot of people will find it very helpful.

5.1

		¹i	n	p	u	t		
²s	c	a	n	n	e	r		
		³b	a	r	c	o	d	e
		⁴s	l	i	d	e	s	
			⁵d	p	i			
⁶h	a	n	d	h	e	l	d	
			⁷p	e	n			
⁸m	e	m	o	r	y			
			⁹f	l	a	t	b	e	d
		¹⁰f	i	l	m			

5.2 1 False. The details detected by a scanner are determined by its resolution.
2 True
3 False. Most scanners can handle optical character recognition.
4 False. A digital camera uses a memory card instead of a light sensitive film for storing the images.
5 False. A digital video (DV) camera is used to record moving images.
6 True

5.3 1 video conferences   4 headset
2 USB   5 webcams
3 frames   6 megapixels

You and computers

Possible answers

1 At home: A scanner lets me scan my favourite photos and manipulate them on my computer. At work: A scanner has transformed the way I work; I capture documents and convert them into editable text using OCR software.

2 My digital camera has a resolution of 7.2 megapixels. It comes with a 3-inch LCD screen and 60 MB of memory and can store up to 160 shots. I take photos and download them to my PC. Then I like to retouch them with photo editing software.
We also have a digital video camera at work. We use it for video conferencing, where several executives of the company are linked together over a network and can see each other and collaborate.
I have a camera phone – a mobile phone which has a built-in camera. It has a resolution of 7 megapixels. I take photos of places and friends. I can also record short video sequences and transmit video calls.

6.1 1 resolution   5 printer
2 dpi, dpi   6 print server
3 printout   7 print spooler
4 pages per minute (ppm)   8 printer driver

6.2 *Suggested answers*

1 ink-jet printer
2 laser printer
3 plotter

4 imagesetter
5 dot-matrix printer

6.3 1 cartridge
2 toner
3 pins

4 impact printing
5 page description language
6 multi-function printer

You and computers

Possible answer

I'd like to have a multi-function ink-jet printer. This type of printer is ideal for my needs because a single machine prints, faxes, copies and scans all sorts of documents, so it's much more economical than buying four separate machines.

My ideal printer is quite fast, with plenty of memory, a high-resolution scanner and a colour fax system. It includes five-colour cartridges, plus black, and produces photo quality colour printing. It's reliable and not very expensive.

I can also contact customer service by telephone or look at an official website, which has support for the printer and driver.

7.1 1 The images shown on a monitor <u>are</u> generated by the video card.
2 All visible colours can be made from mixing the three primary colours of red, <u>green</u> and blue.
3 Typical CRT-based displays occupy <u>more</u> space than LCD displays.
4 Active-matrix LCDs <u>use</u> a technology called thin film transistor or TFT.
5 The size of the screen is measured <u>diagonally</u>.

7.2 1 e   2 b   3 d   4 c   5 a

7.3 1 monitor
2 screen size
3 resolution

4 colour depth
5 brightness

7.4 1 home cinema
2 front-screen projector
3 digital light-processing

4 rear projection
5 plasma display

You and computers

Possible answer

The home cinema of my dreams:

A high-resolution LCD screen, with a 45-inch display mounted on the wall of my living room. The system has a built-in TV tuner and a digital terrestrial television (DTT) receiver which lets me watch hundreds of channels.

Just below the screen there is a DVD recorder with a 200 GB hard drive and a new Blu-ray disc player which I use to record and play back movies.

As for sound capabilities, a Bose Acoustimass system includes five speakers and a subwoofer. An Infrared transmission system enables me to enjoy high-quality surround sound and music without running wires from the front of the room to the rear speakers.

8.1 1 e   2 c   3 f   4 a   5 d   6 b

8.2

```
      ¹c  h  i  ┃p┃ s
   ²b  i  n  a  ┃r┃ y
         ³s  l  ┃o┃ t  s
         ⁴c  l  ┃o┃ c  k
⁵g  i  g  a  h  ┃e┃ r  t  z
         ⁶b  u  ┃s┃ e  s
⁷e  x  p  a  n  ┃s┃ i  o  n
         ⁸b  i  ┃o┃ s
⁹m  o  t  h  e  ┃r┃ b  o  a  r  d
```

8.3
1 It runs at 2.4 GHz.
2 Front Side Bus
3 1,024 MB
4 Yes; RAM can be expanded up to 4 GB

8.4
1 byte
2 kilobyte
3 megabyte
4 gigabyte
5 terabyte

9.1
1 backup
2 floppy disk drive
3 hard disk
4 tracks, sectors
5 access time
6 transfer rate
7 portable hard drive

9.2
1 CD-RW / DVD-RW or DVD+RW
2 CD-R / DVD-R or DVD+R
3 CD-ROM / DVD-ROM
4 flash memory cards (e.g. CompactFlash)
5 flash drive
6 flash memory
7 format a disk

9.3
1 portable DVD player
2 widescreen
3 headphones
4 multi-format playback

You and computers

Possible answers
1 hard disk
2 CD-ROM or DVD-ROM
3 DVD
4 CD, DVD or music player (usually containing flash memory)
5 portable hard drive; DVD-R or DVD-RW discs (to store off-site for security purposes)
6 flash memory card within the camera, and then store the pictures on a CD or flash drive (pen drive) (of course, you can also store your photos on your hard disk)

10.1 1 d 2 c 3 a 4 f 5 g 6 e 7 b

10.2
1 ergonomics
2 repetitive strain injury
3 eye strain
4 recycle, electronic waste
5 mobiles / mobile phones
6 Internet addiction

You and computers

Possible answers

1 There should be adequate space around computers for peripherals, papers, books and other materials.

Make sure computer users can work in a neutral and relaxed typing posture: desks should be the appropriate height; chairs should be adjustable; monitors should be positioned to reduce reflection from lights and windows, using blinds if necessary.

2 The school/college should buy ergonomic ICT equipment. Ergonomic keyboards, mice, copyholders, wrist rests and accessories will help reduce the chance of repetitive strain injury and carpal tunnel syndrome.

3 The location of cables and connectors must minimize the risk of electric shocks. Put cables out of the way so that people don't trip over them.

The use of a wireless network may minimize the risks.

All electrical equipment should be maintained regularly. Technical repairs of computers, network cables, sockets, video projectors, interactive whiteboards, etc. should be done by experts.

4 The school/college should promote good health and safety practice by putting up noticeboards and posters with health and safety recommendations:
• basic information on eye strain, RSI, carpal tunnel syndrome and computer vision problems
• advice on how to use ICT hardware and software correctly and safely
• tips for an ergonomic workstation (seating posture, monitor, keyboard, etc.)
• advice and information on Internet addiction.

11.1
1 System software controls the basic functions of a computer, whereas application software lets you do specific tasks (e.g. writing letters or playing games).
2 Operating system
3 'Multitasking' means running various programs simultaneously.
4 Unix
5 Linux
6 Mac OS
7 Windows
8 Windows, Icons, Menus and Pointer
9 user-friendly

11.2
1 pointer
2 drop-down menu
3 folder
4 window
5 program icon
6 desktop
7 document icon

11.3
1 media player
2 crashed disk rescuer
3 accessibility program
4 compression utility

You and computers

Possible answers

1 Windows is very popular because it's easy to use; everything is presented in graphic images.
2 Some operating systems designed for hand-held devices are: Windows Mobile (Pocket PC), used on most PDAs and smart phones; Palm OS, used on Palm hand-held devices; RIM, used on Blackberry communication devices, developed by Research In Motion.

12.1
1 word processor
2 menu bar
3 typeface
4 header
5 footer
6 layout
7 merge

12.2 1 align left   2 cut and paste   3 undo   4 insert hyperlink   5 graphics

12.3 1 font
2 word wrap
3 Find and replace

4 spell checker
5 thesaurus
6 toolbar

7 Indenting

You and computers

Mercury Robots
49 Charles Place
London SW10 6BA

Phone 020 7385 1541
Fax 020 7385 1390
mercury@tinyworld.co.uk

Mr Vázquez
Alonso Cano, 52
Madrid

(1) Dear Mr Vázquez,
Thank you for your interest in Mercury industrial robots.
(2) Please find enclosed some descriptive leaflets with the technical details of six robots – Cobra and Hercules models. I would like to draw your attention to the *Cobra M2* which is designed for arc welding.
The prices shown in our leaflets are net, but we offer discounts by negotiation. **Mercury Warranty** provides 2-year coverage.
(3) We would be pleased to deliver one of our robot systems on approval, for your inspection.
Please do not hesitate to contact us (4) if you require any further information.
I look forward to hearing from you again soon.
(5) Yours sincerely,

Liz Brown
Sales Office Manager

Help for question 6: how to insert a picture from a Web page.
1 On the Web page, right-click the picture, and then click Copy.
2 In the text document, right-click where you want to insert the picture, and then click Paste.

13.1 1 spreadsheet program
2 column
3 row
4 cell

5 active cell
6 formulae
7 functions

13.2 1 database
2 record
3 field

4 relational
5 index
6 sort

7 query

13.3 1 AutoNumber
2 Text
3 Number

4 Memo
5 OLE Object
6 Yes/No

7 Hyperlink
8 OLE Object
9 Date

You and computers

Possible answers
1 Date, Name and surname, Address, Telephone number, Diagnosis, Treatment, Doctor
2 Author, Title, Date, Publisher, ISBN, Subject, Doc Type, Language, Location

14.1 1 Image manipulation program
2 Business graphics program / presentation software
3 Computer-aided design (CAD)
4 Desktop publishing (DTP)
5 Painting and drawing program / illustration package
6 Geographic information systems (GIS)
7 Computer animation
8 Digital art / computer art

14.2
1	bitmap	3	wireframe	5	clip-art
2	filters	4	Rendering	6	Fractals

14.3
1	Zoom	5	Colour picker	9	Shapes
2	Paintbrush	6	Fill bucket	10	Airbrush
3	Curve	7	Line tool	11	Selection
4	Eraser	8	Pencil	12	Text

You and computers

Possible answers

1 In business, graphics software can be used to:
- make drawings and designs for projects
- generate business graphs and charts. For example, charts can be used to present statistics; a line graph can show how the price of petrol has risen over a number of years, etc.
- make business presentations. Graphics usually convey information more effectively than numbers and text.

2 Computer graphics can be used to develop, model and test car designs before the actual parts are made; this saves money and time. CAD programs are also used to design Formula 1 cars.

3 At home: I use a popular photo and image program called Adobe Photoshop to retouch my favourite photos. I like adding special effects. I sometimes use the software that comes with my digital camera.

15.1 1 hypertext
2 burn music
3 hypermedia
4 .gif (graphics interchange format)
.jpg (jpeg – joint photographic experts group)
.tif (tagged image file)
5 .pdf (portable document format)
.doc (*MS Word* document)
.rtf (rich text format)
.htm / .html (hypertext markup language for the Web)
6 .avi (audio video interleave)
.mov (*QuickTime* movie)
.mpg (mpeg – moving picture experts group)
7 .wav (*Windows* wave audio format)
.ra (*RealAudio* file)
.mp3 (compressed music files)

15.2

			1					
¹a	n	i	m	a	t	i	o	n

²a u d i o
³r e a l i t y
⁴e x t e n s i o n
⁵d i v x
⁶c o m p r e s s
⁷m p e g
⁸v i d e o
⁹g r a p h i c s
¹⁰s t r e a m i n g

Crossword solution:
1 animation
2 audio
3 reality
4 extension
5 divx
6 compress
7 mpeg
8 video
9 graphics
10 streaming

Down: multimedia

15.3
1 consoles   3 graphics   5 Multiplayer
2 Video games   4 interactive

You and computers

Possible answers

1 Yes, I have. For example, I use the *Encarta Encyclopedia*.
  - It is interactive; there are thousands of articles with hyperlinks to other articles.
  - It includes photographs and maps.
  - It also includes sound files and video clips.
  - It has a built-in atlas and dictionary.
2 In a multimedia presentation, the audience is not only informed but also emotionally involved; the message is more memorable.
3 <u>Pros</u> Video and computer games are amusing; they imply mental challenge; you can play online and interact with other people.
  <u>Cons</u> They show violence; they are addictive and create dependence; they may have negative effects on children.

16.1 Across: 1 plug-ins   2 audio   6 fileshare   7 audioblog
Down: 1 podcasting   3 webcasts   4 streaming   5 Internet

16.2
1 MP3 player   4 iPods   7 MP3
2 hard drive   5 built-in / flash   8 ID3
3 memory   6 rip   9 ID3 tags

16.3
1 speech recognition
2 MIDI (musical instrument digital interface)
3 speech synthesis / text-to-speech
4 DAW (digital audio workstation)

17.1 1 c   2 a   3 d   4 b   5 g   6 e   7 f

17.2
1 Analyze the problem   4 Test the program and detect bugs
2 Make flowchart   5 Debug and correct it if necessary
3 Write code and compile   6 Document and maintain the program

17.3
1 dial   4 HTML
2 commands   5 VoiceXML
3 Speech recognition

18.1 a + b network analyst / systems analyst
c + d software engineer / hardware engineer
e + f database administrator / network administrator
g + h help desk technician / trainer

18.2 A technical writer writes documentation of a program or device.
A project manager controls all the operations and people in a project.
A web designer plans and keeps websites updated.
A security specialist designs applications against viruses.

18.3 1 computer operator   2 database analyst

18.4 1 teleworking / telecommuting   4 online teachers
2 teleworkers   5 computer animators
3 telemedicine   6 desktop publishers

You and computers

Possible answers

1 I use a computer to write my projects, letters and documents and print them out. I can store them and use them again or modify them easily. I find and exchange information using the Web. I do online courses.

2 Advantages: independence, no traffic jams or commuting to work
Disadvantages: loneliness, inactive lifestyle, little human contact

19.1 1 software   4 input   7 output
2 hardware   5 processing   8 communication / feedback
3 personnel   6 memory

19.2 1 information system   4 communication system
2 control system   5 information system
3 control system /   6 communication system
communication system

19.3 Across: 1 DAB   3 call   4 Internet   5 fax
Down: 1 digital   2 teletext

You and computers

Possible answers

At home:
I have a PAN (personal area network) with a PDA and a mobile phone to share
and transmit information. I'd like to have a LAN (local area network), with more than one
computer, sharing devices (printers, routers, etc.). I'd like to live in an 'intelligent home' where
different gadgets and sensors are linked and controlled by a central computer.
I have a digital television with lots of channels, which I can interact with in different ways.
I have teletext on the television, with 24-hour information.

We have these at work:
An information system with the database of customers, products, etc.
A WLAN (wireless local area network) where all the computers share information and devices.
A telefax which includes a modem, to send copies of documents via different technologies.
A factory assembly line with robotic elements.

20.1 *Suggested answers*
1 LANs link computers which are near, usually in the same building. / WANs link computers that are placed far apart.
2 In a peer-to-peer architecture, all workstations have the same capabilities. / In a client-server architecture, all the workstations are controlled by one computer.
3 The word protocol refers to the standard of communication between devices in a network. / The word topology refers to the shape of the network.
4 Routers are used to link two networks. / Routers are used to link a LAN to another network.
5 Access points have to be connected to a wired LAN.
6 Wireless adapters are necessary when you are using a WLAN.
7 Hotspots can be found inside and outside buildings.
8 The Internet is an example of a WAN.
9 Wireless WANs use mobile telephone networks as linking devices.

20.2 1 LAN, server   3 nodes   5 backbones
          2 peer-to-peer   4 WLAN   6 hub

20.3 1 star   2 bus   3 tree   4 ring

20.4 a star

You and computers

Possible answers
Advantages: they save money and time; you share hardware; they allow fast access to common files
Disadvantages: there might be a danger of viruses spreading and of hackers accessing the system

21.1 1 False. The WWW is a component of the Internet.
          2 True
          3 True
          4 False. They are two types of broadband connection.
          5 False. They are types of modem.
          6 True
          7 True

21.2 1 mailing list / listserv   5 FTP
          2 TELNET   6 email
          3 video conference   7 Internet telephone
          4 newsgroups   8 chat and instant messaging

21.3 1 wireless   2 broadband   3 modem

22.1 1 attachment   4 username   7 header
          2 snail mail   5 mail server   8 domain name
          3 smileys / emoticons 6 email   9 mailbox

22.2 1 TO   4 subject
          2 signature   5 body
          3 CC
Peter Swinburn's email server is a company (Jazzfree), Mary Jones has a Spanish server and Susan Wilt uses the popular webmail service, Hotmail.

22.3 1 spam   3 spammers   5 email address
          2 newsgroups   4 mailing list

23.1

¹h	i	g	h	w	a	y			

(crossword grid)

¹highway
²hyperlink
³portal
⁴home
⁵blogger
⁶master
⁷spider
⁸index
⁹favourite

The hidden word is 'hypertext'.

23.2

2 web browser
3 URL
4 web server

5 client
6 web page
7 website, surf

8 search engine

23.3

1 weblog / blog
2 cybershopping / e-commerce
3 e-learning

23.4

a protocol (Hypertext Transfer Protocol)
b a resource on the WWW
c domain name
d path
e filename

24.1

Across: 4 WYSIWYG   6 editor   7 template
Down: 1 builder   2 tags   3 source   5 HTML

24.2

1 text
2 background
3 table

4 CSS
5 frame
6 link

7 Graphics
8 JPEG
9 GIF

24.3

1 b   2 d   3 e   4 a   5 c

25.1

1 IRC
2 VoIP
3 VRML
4 dimensional

5 audio
6 chanops
7 client
8 chat

9 applet
10 contact
11 web

25.2

1 chat room
2 messaging, buddy, nicknames
3 avatars
4 video conferencing

26.1

1 piracy, a
2 phishing, f

3 trojan horse, d
4 scam, b

5 worm, e
6 cyberstalking, c

26.2

1 malware
2 digital certificate
3 firewall

4 spyware
5 virus
6 antivirus

7 scanner

You and computers

Possible answers

1

I don't open email attachments unless I'm sure I know who's sending them.

I never buy illegal programs.

I back up my files.

I don't download music from Internet websites I don't trust.

I don't copy programs.

I never trust email messages with wonderful offers or those that ask for personal details (bank account number, credit card, etc.).

2

I always keep my virus protection updated.

There are hundreds of websites where free advice can be found and even some downloadable antivirus programs. Here are some examples:

http://securityresponse.symantec.com/

http://www.f-secure.com/

http://www.sophos.com/security/

http://vil.nai.com/vil/default.aspx

http://www.microsoft.com/security/antivirus/default.mspx

To improve your computer security you should buy or download from the Web an antivirus program and make sure you keep it updated.

Your computer system should have a firewall.

27.1 Across: **1** shopping   **5** B2C   **7** e-commerce
Down: **1** SSL   **2** online   **3** gateway   **4** B2B   **6** C2C

27.2 **1** c (comparison engine)   **4** a (log in / sign up)
2 f (basket / cart)   **5** e (account)
3 b (checkout)   **6** d (log out)

27.3 **1** Online shopping   **3** auctions
2 dotcoms, bricks and clicks   **4** digital wallet

You and computers

Possible answers

Any shopping directory, e.g. www.shopsafe.co.uk, will include all types of services from alcoholic drinks to travel agencies, clothes, furniture, etc.

28.1 **1** brick-and-click banks   **4** online banking / Internet banking
2 wireless banking   **5** brick-and-mortar banks
3 virtual banks / Internet banks   **6** electronic banking

28.2 **1** trade   **3** check   **5** funds   **7** send
2 pay   **4** online statements   **6** payments

28.3 **1** two-factor   **3** security token   **5** transaction authorization number
2 PIN   **4** biometric

You and computers

Possible answers

2

Advantages:

It's very convenient: you can do transactions any time, anywhere, with just a computer or a mobile phone plus Internet connection.

You can reduce your banking fees.

You save time.

There is no waste of paper (envelopes, statements, etc.).

Disadvantages:
If you need cash, you will need an ATM or a brick-and-mortar bank.
You need to remember your password.
You may miss the human contact with a friendly bank clerk.
You must be absolutely sure the online institution offers a secure connection.

29.1
1 cellular phones	4 coverage
2 cells	5 range
3 base stations	6 roaming

29.2
1 True
2 False. They introduced digital technology.
3 False. It started to be used in the 90s.
4 True
5 False. People will be able to watch live TV on 4G phones.
6 True
7 True

29.3 1 c 2 d 3 b 4 e 5 a

30.1
1 sensors	4 actuator	7 computer system
2 end effector	5 robot	
3 joints	6 automata	

30.2
1 mobile robot	3 surgical robot	5 robotic arm
2 planetary rover	4 space probe	

30.3
1 Artificial Intelligence	3 Neural networks
2 androids	4 Expert systems

You and computers

Possible answers
Cleaning robots, lawn-mowing robots, robotic guides, deep sea explorers, help desk technicians, etc.

31.1 Across: 3 Bluetooth 6 interfaces 7 wireless 9 initiator
Down: 1 automation 2 robotics 4 intelligent 5 receiver 7 wired 8 PAN

31.2
1 Security, safety, comfort and economy. There is no reference to assistive technology.
2 It can turn lights on and off, control the heating, control security and safety systems, detect problems and act accordingly, e.g. tell the owner to phone a plumber.
3 The main interface is a mobile phone. There is an information and control system in the house that receives instructions from the phone.
In the future, the home will respond to voice commands.

32.1
1 DNA computer	3 Nanotechnology	5 nanocomputer
2 quantum computer	4 nanobots	

32.2
1 immersive Internet	4 intelligent robot
2 mobile TV	5 RFID – radio frequency identification tags
3 wearable computer	6 gesture interface

32.3 1 d 2 a 3 e 4 c 5 b

33.1
1 teleconferencing
2 Non-volatile
3 supersites
4 Semiconductors
5 intranet
6 interconnected

33.2
1 unformatted
2 extranet
3 transmission
4 reboot
5 microbrowser

33.3
1 <u>un</u>install
2 <u>en</u>crypted
3 <u>de</u>crypted
4 <u>de</u>compresses
5 <u>de</u>bug
6 <u>up</u>load
7 <u>up</u>date
8 <u>de</u>fragment
9 <u>up</u>grade

33.4
1 cyberspace
2 cyberslacking
3 e-zines
4 e-commerce
5 e-learning

You and computers

Possible answers
cyberculture: the culture related to the use of computer networks in communication; cyberculture has its own customs and etiquette
cybersquatting: when someone registers a famous name as an Internet address, so that they can sell it later at a high price to the person or organization with that name
cybercrime: criminal offences committed against or with the help of computer networks
cyberattack: an assault against a network or computer system
cybercast: using the Web to broadcast information or entertainment
e-card: an electronic card, digital card or postcard created on the Web and sent to somebody via the Web
e-calling: making telephone calls from your computer; synonymous with IP telephony
e-cash: electronic cash, digital money provided by a special bank, which can be used to buy goods and services from online shops which accept this form of payment
e-book: an electronic book, a book that is published in electronic form, for example on the Internet or on a disc, and not printed on paper
e-signature: a set of electronic symbols used or authorized by an individual to be the legally binding equivalent of the individual's handwritten signature (A digital signature is an electronic signature which uses some form of encryption to ensure that the identity of the signer can be verified.)

34.1
1 software engineer
2 computer consultant
3 animator
4 typist
5 manufacturer
6 computer technician

34.2
1 powerful
2 accessible
3 attachment
4 computerize
5 erasable
6 security
7 electronics
8 wireless
9 simulation

34.3
1 magnetism
2 magnetic
3 recorder
4 recordable
5 digitizer
6 digitally

34.4
1 spyware
2 shareware
3 malware
4 adware
5 groupware
6 freeware

35.1
1 silicon chip
2 web portal
3 control panel
4 recording head
5 address bus

35.2
1 Mail merge
2 add-on
3 self-test
4 search engine
5 software engineer

35.3 Across: 1 setup / set-up   4 scrollbar   5 clipboard   6 broadband
Down: 1 shortcut   2 smartcard / smart card   3 bandwidth

35.4

1 voice-activated
2 stand-alone
3 menu-driven
4 hands-free
5 object-oriented
6 space-saving

36.1

1 d 2 e 3 c 4 a 5 h 6 b 7 f 8 g

36.2

1 wireless hotspots
2 plug and play
3 hacking into a computer
4 drag and drop
5 highly sensitive

36.3

1 outgoing
2 instant, install, into
3 CDs
4 stream
5 real
6 freely
7 onto

36.4

1 Internet
2 electronic
3 virtual
4 high-speed
5 data
6 online
7 interactive
8 emails
9 Web

37.1

1 b 2 d 3 a 4 e 5 c

37.2

1 that / which
2 who
3 where
4 that / which

37.3

A computer <u>consists of</u> hardware and software.
... <u>constitute</u> what is known as hardware ...
... <u>are the basic parts of</u> the CPU.
The RAM and the ROM <u>make up</u> the main memory.
Peripherals <u>are classified into three types</u>: ...
Software <u>can be divided into two categories</u>: ...
... which <u>includes</u> operating systems, ...
... which <u>comprises</u> programs that ...

37.4

1 There are four main classes of
2 are made up of
3 is composed of
4 There are two types of
5 is a type of

You and computers

Possible answer

38.1

1 highly demanding
2 high-end
3 fast
4 plentiful
5 low-end
6 expandable

38.2

1 spacious
2 separate, integrated
3 compatible
4 reliable

38.3
1 Both	6 slimmer	11 as
2 similar	7 Unlike	12 best
3 While	8 as well as	13 the
4 more	9 more	
5 than	10 but	

39.1 1 converted, digitized, processed   2 displayed   3 fed

39.2 Across: 1 customized   6 uploaded   8 hooked   9 held
Down: 2 upgraded   3 threaded   4 defragmented   5 set   7 posted

39.3 1 d   2 b   3 a   4 f   5 c   6 e

You and computers

Possible answer
First the computer must be switched on. Once the OS has booted up, you can run the word processor. Then the document is typed in. It can be edited: for example, graphics can be inserted. Next the file should be saved before it is printed. Finally, your computer should be switched off.

40.1
1 error message / dialogue box	3 help desk
2 debugging	4 help desk technician / troubleshooting

40.2 1 i   2 d   3 b   4 g   5 e   6 a   7 c   8 h   9 f

40.3
1 cooling fan	4 back up
2 UPS (uninterruptible power supply)	5 turn
3 recovery tool	6 reboot

You and computers

Possible answers
My computer displayed an error message.
The monitor flickered.
I lost some important files.
I wasn't able to connect to the Internet.
The computer was affected by a virus.
It ran short of memory.
The monitor showed a blue screen with a warning message.

Index

The numbers in the index are **Unit** numbers not page numbers.

Acronyms are pronounced as individual letters where no pronunciation is shown, e.g. ADSL.

make a backup /ˌmeɪk ə 'bækʌp/ 9

make calculations /ˌmeɪk kælkjʊ'leɪʃənz/ 1

malware (malicious software) /'mælweəʳ/ 26, 34

manufacturer /mænjʊ'fæktʃərəʳ/ 34

markup language /'mɑːkʌp ˌlæŋgwɪdʒ/ 17

media player /'miːdiə ˌpleɪəʳ/ 11

megabyte /'megəbaɪt/ 8

megapixel /'megəpɪksəl/ 5

memo /'meməʊ/ 13

memory /'memᵊri/ 19

menu bar /'menjuː ˌbɑːʳ/ 12

menu-driven /'menjuːdrɪvᵊn/ 35

merge /mɜːdʒ/ 12 See also mail merge

microbrowser /'maɪkrəʊˌbraʊzəʳ/ 33

microphone /'maɪkrəfəʊn/ 4

MIDI (musical instrument digital interface) /'mɪdi/ 16, 24

MIPS (millions of instructions per second) /mɪps/ 32

mobile phone /ˌməʊbaɪl 'fəʊn/ 29 See also cell phone

mobile robots /ˌməʊbaɪl 'rəʊbɒts/ 30

mobile TV /ˌməʊbaɪl tiː'viː/ 32

modem (modulator-demodulator /'məʊdem/ 2, 21

monitor /'mɒnɪtəʳ/ 2, 7

monitor at eye level /'mɒnɪtər ət aɪ levᵊl/ 10

motherboard /'mʌðəbɔːd/ 8

mouse /maʊs/ 2, 4

MP3 (MPEG audio layer 3) 16, 24, 29

MP3 player /empiː'θriː ˌpleɪəʳ/ 16

multi-format playback /'mʌltifɔːmæt 'pleɪbæk/ 9

multi-function printer / mʌltiˌfʌŋkʃən 'prɪntəʳ/ 6

multimedia /ˌmʌlti'miːdiə/ 15

multimedia file / mʌltiˌmiːdiə 'faɪl/ 24

multiplayer /'mʌltiˌpleɪəʳ/ 15

multitasking /ˌmʌlti'tɑːskɪŋ/ 11

nanobot /'nænəʊbɒt/ 32

nanocomputer /ˌnænəʊkəm'pjuːtəʳ/ 32

nanotechnology /ˌnænəʊtek'nɒlədʒi/ 32

network analyst /ˌnetwɜːk 'ænəlɪst/ 18

network connection refused by server /ˌnetwɜːk kə'nekʃən rɪf'juːzd baɪ ˌsɜːvəʳ/ 40

network / computer systems administrator /ˌnetwɜːk/ kəmˌpjuːtə ˌsɪstəmz əd'mɪnɪstreɪtəʳ/ 18

networking /'netwɜːkɪŋ/ 20

neural network /ˌnjʊərᵊl 'netwɜːk/ 30

newsgroup /'njuːzgruːp/ 21, 22

nickname /'nɪkneɪm/ 25

node /nəʊd/ 20

non-volatile /ˌnɒn'vɒlətaɪl/ 33

Not Found /ˌnɒt 'faʊnd/ 40

notebook PC /ˌnəʊtbʊk piː'siː/ 3

number /'nʌmbəʳ/ 13

numeric keypad /njuːˌmerɪk 'kiːpæd/ 4

object-oriented /ˌɒbdʒɪkt'ɔːriəntɪd/ 35

OLE Object /ˌəʊleɪ 'ɒbdʒɪkt/ 13

online banking /ˌɒnlaɪn 'bæŋkɪŋ/ 28

online shop /ˌɒnlaɪn 'ʃɒp/ 27

online shopping /ˌɒnlaɪn 'ʃɒpɪŋ/ 27

online teacher /ˌɒnlaɪn 'tiːtʃəʳ/ 18

online telephone conversation /ˌɒnlaɪn 'telɪfəʊn kɒnvəˌseɪʃᵊn/ 25

operating system /'ɒpəreɪtɪŋ ˌsɪstəm/ 11

optical character recognition /ˌɒptɪkᵊl 'kærəktə rekəgˌnɪʃᵊn/ 5

optical disc /ˌɒptɪkᵊl 'dɪsk/ 36

outgoing mail /ˌaʊtgəʊɪŋ 'meɪl/ 36

out of range /ˌaʊt əv 'reɪndʒ/ 29

output /'aʊtpʊt/ 2, 19

output devices /'aʊtpʊt dɪˌvaɪsɪz/ 2

page description language /ˌpeɪdʒ dɪ'skrɪpʃᵊn ˌlæŋgwɪdʒ/ 6

pages per minute (ppm) /ˌpeɪdʒɪz pə 'mɪnɪt/ 6

paintbrush /'peɪntbrʌʃ/ 14

painting and drawing program /ˌpeɪntɪŋ ən 'drɔːɪŋ ˌprəʊgræm/ 14

PAN (personal area network) /pæn/ 31

paste /peɪst/ 12

path /pɑːθ/ 23

pay bills /ˌpeɪ 'bɪlz/ 28

payment gateway /'peɪmənt ˌgeɪtweɪ/ 27

PC card /piː'si ˌkɑːd/ 21

PDA (personal digital assistant) 3, 29

peer-to-peer /ˌpɪətəpɪəʳ/ 20

pencil /'pensᵊl/ 14

pen scanner /'pen ˌskænəʳ/ 5

peripheral /pə'rɪfᵊrᵊl/ 2, 5

personnel /pɜːsᵊn'el/ 19

phishing /'fɪʃɪŋ/ 26

phosphor /'fɒsfəʳ/ 7

PIN (personal identification number) /pɪn/ 28

pins /pɪnz/ 6

piracy /'paɪrəsi/ 26

pixels /'pɪksᵊlz/ 7

planetary rover /ˌplænətri 'rəʊvəʳ/ 30

plasma display /ˌplæzmə dɪ'spleɪ/ 7

play videos and music /'pleɪ 'vɪdiəʊz ən 'mjuːzɪk/ 36

plentiful /'plentɪfʊl/ 38

plotter /'plɒtəʳ/ 6

plug and play /ˌplʌg ən 'pleɪ/ 36

plug-in /'plʌgɪn/ 16, 24

plug into the computer /ˌplʌg 'ɪntuː ðə kəm'pjuːtəʳ/ 36

podcast /'pɒdkɑːst/ 16

podcasting /'pɒdkɑːstɪŋ/ 16

pointer /'pɔɪntəʳ/ 11

portable DVD player /ˌpɔːtəbᵊl diːviː'diː ˌpleɪəʳ/ 9

portable hard drive /ˌpɔːtəbᵊl 'hɑːd ˌdraɪv/ 9

port /pɔːt/ 2, 3

post /pəʊst/ 39

spoken tutorial /ˌspəʊkən
tjuːˈtɔːriəl/ 16

spreadsheet /ˈspredʃiːt/ 13

spyware /ˈspaɪweər/ 26, 34

stand-alone /ˈstændəˌləʊn/ 35

star /stɑːr/ 20

storage /ˈstɔːrɪdʒ/ 2

storage devices /ˈstɔːrɪdʒ
dɪˌvaɪsɪz/ 2

store information /ˌstɔːr
ɪnfəˈmeɪʃən/ 1

stream files /ˈstriːm ˌfaɪlz/ 36

streaming /ˈstriːmɪŋ/ 15, 16

stylus /ˈstaɪləs/ 3

SUBJECT /ˈsʌbdʒekt/ 22

supersite /ˈsuːpəsaɪt/ 33

surf /sɜːf/ 23

surf the Web /ˌsɜːf ðə ˈweb/ 1

surgical robot /ˌsɜːdʒɪkəl
ˈrəʊbɒt/ 30

system software /ˌsɪstəm
ˈsɒftweər/ 11

systems analyst /ˈsɪstəmz
ˌænəlɪst/ 18

table /ˈteɪbəl/ 24

tablet PC /ˌtæblət piːˈsiː/ 3

TAN (transaction authorization
number) /tæn/ 28

TCP / IP (Transmission Control
Protocol / Internet Protocol)
21

technical writer /ˈteknɪkəl ˌraɪtər/
18

technological dependence /
teknəˌlɒdʒɪkəl dɪˈpendənts/ 1

teleconferencing
/ˌtelɪˈkɒnfərəntsɪŋ/ 33

telemedicine /ˌtelɪˈmedsən/ 18

telephone line /ˈtelɪfəʊn ˌlaɪn/
21

teletext /ˈtelɪtekst/ 19

teleworking / telecommuting
/ˈtelɪwɜːkɪŋ /
ˌtelɪkəˈmjuːtɪŋ/ 18

teleworker /ˈtelɪwɜːkər/ 18

TELNET /ˈtelnet/ 21

terabyte /ˈterəbaɪt/ 8

test /test/ 17

text /tekst/ 13, 14, 24

text-to-speech /ˌteksttəˈspiːtʃ/
16

TFT screen /tiːefˈtiː skriːn/ 3

thesaurus /θɪˈsɔːrəs/ 12

Third Generation (3G) /ˌθɜːd
dʒenəˈreɪʃən/ 29

thread /θred/ 39

three-dimensional (3D)
/ˌθriːdaɪˈmenʃənəl/ 25

TO /tuː/ 22

toner /ˈtəʊnər/ 6

toolbar /ˈtuːlbɑːr/ 12

top-level domain /ˌtɒplevəl
dəˈmeɪn/ 22

topology /tɒˈpɒlədʒi/ 20

touch screen /ˈtʌtʃ ˌskriːn/ 3, 4

touchpad /ˈtʌtʃpæd/ 3, 4

track /træk/ 9

trackball /ˈtrækbɔːl/ 4

trade stocks /ˈtreɪd ˌstɒks/ 28

transfer rate /ˈtræntsfɜːr ˌreɪt/ 9

transfer the funds /ˌtræntsfɜː
ðə ˈfʌnds/ 28

transmission /trænzˈmɪʃən/ 33

transmit data /ˌtrænzmɪt ˈdeɪtə/
36

tree /triː/ 20

trojan horse /ˌtrəʊdʒən ˈhɔːs/ 26

troubleshooting /ˈtrʌblˌʃuːtɪŋ/
40

tune in to Internet radio /tjuːn
in tə ˌintənet ˈreɪdiəʊ/ 36

turn off /ˌtɜːn ˈɒf/ 40

two-factor authentication
/ˌtuːfæktər ɔːˈθentɪkeɪʃən/ 28

typeface /ˈtaɪpfeɪs/ 12

typist /ˈtaɪpɪst/ 34

UMTS (Universal Mobile
Telecommunications System)
29

unauthorized /ʌnˈɔːθəraɪzd/ 40

undo /ʌnˈduː/ 12

unformatted /ʌnˈfɔːmætɪd/ 33

uninstall /ʌnɪnˈstɔːl/ 33

Unix /ˈjuːnɪks/ 11

update /ʌpˈdeɪt/ 33

upgrade /ʌpˈgreɪd/ 33, 39

upload /ʌpˈləʊd/ 33, 39

UPS (uninterruptible power
supply) 40

URL (Uniform Resource
Locator) 23

USB 5

USB port /juːesˈbiː ˌpɔːt/ 3

use of mobiles /ˌjuːs əv
ˈməʊbaɪlz/ 10

user interface /ˌjuːzər ˈɪntəfeɪs/
32

user-friendly /ˌjuːzəˈfrendli/ 11

username /ˈjuːzəneɪm/ 22

vector graphic /ˈvektə ˌgræfɪk/
14

video /ˈvɪdiəʊ/ 15, 25

video card /ˈvɪdiəʊ ˌkɑːd/ 7

video console /ˌvɪdiəʊ
ˈkɒnsəʊl/ 15

video editing software /ˈvɪdiəʊ
ˌedɪtɪŋ ˌsɒftweər/ 5

video game /ˈvɪdiəʊ ˌgeɪm/ 15

video conference /ˌvɪdiəʊ
ˈkɒnfərənts/ 5, 21

video conferencing /ˌvɪdiəʊ
ˈkɒnfərəntsɪŋ/ 25

virtual bank /ˌvɜːtʃuəl ˈbæŋk/
28

virtual environment /ˌvɜːtʃuəl
ɪnˈvaɪərənmənt/ 36

virtual reality /ˌvɜːtʃuəl
riˈæləti/ 1, 15

virus /ˈvaɪrəs/ 26, 40

voice recognition /ˈvɔɪs
rekəgˌnɪʃən/ 3

voice-recognition system /ˌvɔɪs
rekəgˈnɪʃən ˌsɪstəm/ 4

voice-activated
/ˌvɔɪsˈæktɪveɪtɪd/ 35

VoiceXML /ˌvɔɪseksemˈel/ 17

VoIP (Voice over Internet
Protocol) /vɔɪp/ 25

VRML (Virtual Reality
Modelling Language) 25

WAN (Wide Area Network)
/wæn/ 20

WAP (Wireless Application
Protocol) /wæp/ 29

WAV /wæv/ 24

wearable computer /ˌweərəbl
kəmˈpjuːtər/ 3, 32

web browser /ˈweb ˌbraʊzər/ 23

web chat /ˈweb ˌtʃæt/ 25

Describing function 37

a <u>device</u> **used to** transmit

a <u>device</u> **for** transmit**ting**

a <u>device</u> **which/that** transmits

a <u>device</u> **which/that is used to** transmit

a <u>person</u> **who** …

the <u>area</u> **where** …

Classifying 37

… **are classified into** X types/ categories

… **can be divided into** X types/ categories

… **include**

… **consists of**

… **is made up of**

… **is composed of**

… **comprise**

there are X **types of** …

there are X **classes of** …

there are X **categories of** …

… **is a type of**

… **are parts of**

… **are components of**

… **constitute**

… **make up**

Comparison 38

as good as

less money

more quality **than**

more manageable **than**

more easily

slimmer **than**

the more memory … **the** faster

the best

Contrast 38

but

unlike

while

Similarity 38

as well as

similar

both … **and** …

Passive verbs 39

be converted

be customized

be defragmented

be digitized

be displayed

be fed into

be held

be hooked up

be posted

be processed

be set up

be threaded

be upgraded

be uploaded

Acknowledgements

The authors and publishers would like to thank the following for permission to reproduce copyright texts, photographs and other illustrative material. While every effort has been made, it has not always been possible to identify the sources of all the material used, or to contact the copyright holders. If any omissions are brought to our notice, we will be happy to include the appropriate acknowledgements on reprinting.

Texts

pp. 10, 11, 92 dictionary entries from *Cambridge Advanced Learner's Dictionary*, edited by P. Gillard, published by Cambridge University Press; *Miami Herald* for the text on p. 10 taken from 'Birth of a Revolution', 5 August 2001, bgarcia@herald.com; Microsoft product screenshots on pp. 12, 32, 34, 35, 38, 40 reprinted with permission from Microsoft Corporation; Creative Labs (UK) Ltd for the adapted text on p. 21, taken from WebCam Live! Ultra from www.creative.com; Atlantic Electronics for the specification on p. 29 for the Panasonic DVD-LS91, 9 inch portable DivX DVD player taken from www.atlantic2u.net; Apple screenshot on p. 33 reproduced with permission of Apple Computer Inc.; VNU for the adapted text on p. 37, 'A database is essentially nothing more than a computerised record-keeping system', *Personal Computer World*, 1 May 1997, © VNU Business Publications, 1995–2006. All rights reserved; *Slate* for the adapted text on p. 41 from 'Video Games' by Eliza Truitt, Slate Magazine, 30 September 1998, www.slate.com; *The Herald* for the adapted text on p. 42 from 'Why iPod isn't the only player', 25 August 2004, © 2006 Newsquest (Herald and Times) Limited. All rights reserved; *The Economist* for the text on p. 45, adapted from 'Internet: voice recognition takes off', 13 May 2000, © The Economist Newspaper Limited 2006; *The Mirror* for the adapted texts on p. 53, 'Grab a fair share of the Internet', 19 July 2003, on p. 55, 'How to junk rogue email', 28 June 2003, on pp. 62–3, 'How to fight fraudsters', 6 October 2004, and on p. 64, 'Money, the key to safe cyber shopping', © Mirror Group Newspapers Ltd; Tamora James for the web page and raw HTML code on p. 58; CNN for the adapted text on p. 73, '"Smart" homes are not far away', 31 May 2005, © 2006 Cable News Network LP, LLLP; Learn The Net for the text on p. 83 taken from 'A new kind of web', www.learnthenet.com.

Photos and cartoons

(Key: t = top; c = centre; b = bottom; l = left; r = right)

Alamy pp. 10 (ImageState), 12r (Nikreates), 30b (WoodyStock), 38b (Dennis Hallinan), 46 (Profimedia International s.r.o.), 71tc (photolibrary), 86b (Tony Cordoza), 90 (ImageState); Courtesy of Encyclopaedia Britannica Inc. p. 40b; CartoonStock.com pp. 13br (Deacon), 19b (Chris Wildt), 23 (Mike Flanagan), 33b (Noel Ford), 49 (Fran), 51 (Aaron Bacall), 55 (Irfan), 63 (Rob Baines), 65 (Mike Baldwin), 67 (Harley Schwadron), 73 (Mike Baldwin), 79 (Andrew Toos); Corbis pp. 24b (Naljah Feanny), 64t (Digital Art); By permission of Larry Ewing, lewing@isc.tamu.edu and The GIMP p. 32t; Elena Marco Fabré and Santiago Remacha Esteras p. 38cr; Courtesy of Nathan Galli and Chris Johnson, SCI Institute p. 75tl; Getty Images pp. 13l (Ken Reid), 13r (ML Harris), 17b (Altrendo), 68b (Junko Sato/Neovision), 70b (Junko Kimura), 71tl (Ed Darack), 75tc (Valery Hache), 80 (Yoshikazu Tsuno/AFP), 82r (Toshifumi Kitamura); Randy Glasbergen, www.glasbergen.com p. 29b; The Kobal Collection p. 75bl (20th Century Fox); Courtesy of Nokia p. 82l; Courtesy of Panasonic p. 29t; Punchstock pp. 60c, 77, 86t; Rex Features p. 75bc (Sipa Press); Science Photo Library pp. 30c (Jerry Mason), 39 (Alfred Pasieka), 70cb (Alfred Pasieka), 71tr (Pascal Goetghluck), 71bl (NASA), 71br (Maximilian Stock Ltd), 74t (Coneyl Jay), 75tr (Sam Ogden), 83 (David Parker); Courtesy of Toshiba p. 17t; Courtesy of University of Washington Medical Center Rehabilitation Counseling p. 13c; Courtesy of J. P. Wachs, Institute for Medical Informatics, Washington DC p. 75br.

Photographs sourced by Suzanne Williams, www.Pictureresearch.co.uk

Illustrations by Celia Canning pp. 34, 62, 74; Peter Cornwell pp. 12, 42, 48, 54, 57, 58; Mark Duffin pp. 12, 13, 14, 16, 18, 19, 20, 21, 22, 24, 25, 26, 27, 28, 30, 31, 36, 42, 50, 52, 57, 60, 64, 66, 68, 69, 70, 72, 76, 78, 81, 84, 88, 89; Roger Harris p. 70